190 Cub Scouts from Newham, East London, had a great day visiting the Bluebell Line Railway which runs between Horsted Keynes and Sheffield Park in Sussex. *See colour feature on pages 45 and 46.*

CONTENTS

Published in Great Britain by World Distributors (Manchester) Limited,
P.O. Box 111, 12 Lever Street, Manchester M60 1TS.
Printed and bound by Morrison & Gibb Ltd, Edinburgh.
SBN 7235 0206 4

Editor's note:
Contributions for future issues of this Annual should be sent to:
The General Editor, The Scout Association,
25 Buckingham Palace Road,
London, SW1W 0PY

While every reasonable care is taken of all MSS, Typescripts, Drawings, Photographs, etc., submitted, no liability can be accepted for loss or damage to any such material through any cause whatever. Material can only be returned if a stamped, addressed envelope is sent.

the cub scout

ANNUAL 1974

Edited by RON JEFFRIES

General Editor of The Scout Association and Editor of SCOUTING Magazine

Assisted by CLAIRE WYATT

THE SNOWSTORM

Michael and his younger brother John were both in the Cubs, and as part of their Christmas good turn they had taken presents and food to their Aunt Joan who lived in a tiny village called Chalfont. They had walked across the moors to get to the village, but when they arrived at Aunt Joan's cottage they found that she was not there. So they knocked on the door of a nearby cottage and the old lady living there told them that their aunt had gone to stay with some relatives for Christmas. However the old lady was very kind, and she took them inside and gave them a hot drink and something to eat. She also offered to look after the presents and give them to Aunt Joan when she came back, so their journey was not completely wasted.

A little later, at about four o'clock, Michael and John thanked the old lady for the food and drink, and told her that they would have to be leaving as they had an hour's walk ahead of them. They put on their coats and caps and slung their empty satchels over their shoulders and left, waving to the old lady as they went.

They had only walked a short distance when John felt something wet blow against his face. He looked up and then shouted, "Look, Mike, it's snowing. Isn't that great? We're going to have a white Christmas after all."

Although Michael was just as pleased as his brother to see the snow, he hoped that it would not fall any harder before they got home, because he knew how cold it could get on the moors. But he didn't mention this when he spoke. "Just think, we may be able to get the toboggan out again, like we did last year. But come on, let's hurry home first, in case Mum starts to worry."

So they speeded up and were soon over the first hill with the village behind them out of sight. As they plodded along the moorland path, Michael became more and more worried,

because the snow was falling much harder now and, even worse, a strong wind had started to blow. However, there was nothing they could do but keep going, and on they went with snow swirling around their faces and their hands becoming colder and colder.

John put his hand on Michael's arm and spoke in a shaky voice: "How much further have we got to go? I'm getting so cold and we seem to have been walking for ages. Can't we stop somewhere and rest?"

"It's all right, there's no need to worry, we'll soon be home," said Michael in a confident voice, but he wished that he felt as confident as he sounded.

He looked at his watch, it was five minutes past five, which meant that they had been walking for over an hour now, and they should have reached the road that led to their own village.

Suddenly he became scared. He realised that they must have wandered from the path. It would not have been difficult to do, because even though he had tried his best to follow it, his eyes could easily have been tricked by the swirling snow. They could have strayed onto another path, but he realised that whatever had happened there was still nothing they could do except press on in the hope that they came across a cottage or village.

He decided not to tell John for a while, so that he wouldn't be too frightened.

The snow on the ground was getting thicker and it was getting more difficult to walk along, especially for John, who was panting for breath and holding on to Michael's arm for support.

Suddenly, Michael stopped, holding John's arm. "Listen, I thought I heard something," he said.

They both listened. Through the noise of the wind they both heard a cry for help.

"Did you hear where it was coming from?" asked John. "It couldn't have been from very far away."

"Yes, I think that it came from up ahead somewhere. Come on, let's see if we can find who's calling." Summoning their remaining strength they hurried on.

Twice more they heard the cry for help, then John shouted excitedly: "Look, over there! Isn't that a light?"

Michael peered through the snow, but could see nothing. Then suddenly he spotted it. "You're right, I think it must be from a cottage."

When they got nearer they could see that it was a cottage. They saw that the light was coming from the open front door, and standing there was an old woman, wrapped in a thick blanket. When she saw Michael and John approaching through the snow to the door, she shouted to them in a feeble voice: "Please help me, please. My husband is ill, and I've been praying for someone to come." And with that she stepped back into the cottage to let them in.

For a few moments they were both so dazed with the peace and quiet of the cottage compared with the storm outside that they hadn't realised that the old woman was nowhere to be seen. Michael walked through the door ahead of him and saw the old woman spread out on the settee in front of the fire. It took him a minute to get his breath back, and then he spoke to his brother.

"Gosh, she looks frozen, doesn't she? I wonder how long she's been standing there? She must be exhausted, she's sleeping already. I think that it would be best to leave her where she is, don't you?"

But there was no answer from John; he too

was exhausted from walking through the raging storm. Michael looked at him and spoke again.

"Hey, you look worn out yourself. Come over here and sit down by the fire and try to get warm. You'll soon feel better. I'll see if I can find any blankets to help keep the lady warm."

So John sat down in an armchair, leaning towards the fire to try and get some warmth into his shivering body, while Michael looked round the cottage.

Then from one of the rooms he heard a groan. Suddenly, he remembered. As the old lady had let them come into the cottage she had said that her husband was ill. He opened the door of the room quietly and looked in. He saw the man lying in bed groaning, and he went in, letting the man see him so that he would not be startled.

The man tried to sit up, but he fell back on the bed.

There was silence for a short while, then the man spoke, in a voice weak with pain: "Thank God someone has come. I need a doctor, son, quickly. Try and get one for me. I know that it won't be easy in this storm, but try your best." And with that he drifted off into a deep sleep.

Michael didn't know what was wrong with the man, but it was obvious that he needed a doctor as soon as possible, snowstorm or no snowstorm. He saw some blankets on top of a wardrobe and so he climbed on to a chair and took some off the pile and carried them into the front room.

John was much better now that he had warmed up and so he helped Michael to wrap the blankets around the old lady. When they had finished Michael stood quietly for a

moment, thinking about what he was going to do. He realised that there was really only one thing, and that was for him to go out into the storm again to try and get some help. He knew that it would be dangerous, but he couldn't let the man in the bedroom suffer without trying to do something. Finally he made up his mind.

"Look," he said to John. "I'm going to have to try to get some help. I want you to stay here and look after the lady and the man in the bedroom. If the lady wakes up give her a nice hot cup of tea and tell her that help is on the way. Don't worry too much about the old man, he's sleeping at the moment and I don't think he'll wake up. Do you think that you'll be all right?"

"I'll be all right," John replied, a little shakily. "But do you have to go? I'd much rather you stayed here."

"Yes, I must go, so that I can get a doctor. I'll be as quick as I can."

John nodded glumly and turned away.

Michael had one more thing to do before he left. He would have to find the address of the cottage, as he didn't have any idea of where he was, and it wouldn't be much good if he managed to get help but didn't know where to send them. In the corner of the room was a writing desk, and so he went over to it and looked for any letters that were there. He found a pile addressed to the cottage and so he took the first one and put it in his pocket.

Then he went to the front door, turning as he reached it to call to John, who was following him out of the room: "Cheerio, don't worry. I won't be long, the time will soon pass."

He put on his gloves and cap and was then out in the snow once more, with the door shut behind him. By this time, of course, it was dark outside, which made it even more frightening to be in the storm alone. The wind was still as strong and the snow was falling as hard as ever. However, at least this time he was on a road and there was little chance of him wandering from it, as it was lined on both sides by hedges.

Soon his feet and hands were freezing cold again, and he began to wish that he had stayed at the cottage after all. But the thought of the poor old man lying in bed kept him going, step by step through the ever-thickening layer of snow on the ground. After a while the

snow was so deep that it came over the tops of his shoes, making his socks and feet wet and even colder.

Mile after mile he walked without seeing or hearing any signs of life, except for the occasional sound of sheep bleating in some of the fields that he passed. All the time the wind was blowing the snow down his neck and against his face, so that his whole body became numb with the bitter cold.

Once he thought that he saw a light up ahead, but he soon realised that it was just the swirling snow playing tricks on his eyes. So he went on plodding through the storm, becoming more and more frightened as he got colder and more tired.

Then, to his joy, he heard the sound of a dog barking, and he knew that he must be near a village or at least a cottage. He pressed on with renewed strength and a few yards further along the road he saw the name sign of a village.

He went up to it and rubbed off the snow so that he could read it. When the name became clear he just stared at the sign for a full minute. Then he blinked his eyes hard and stared again.

He just couldn't believe his eyes, for there was the name of his own village, and that meant that his own house was only a few hundred yards along the road.

With his heart beating madly with relief and excitement, he managed to summon enough energy to run through the snow. He slipped once, but he got straight up and raced on, and soon he had reached his own front door.

He banged on it wildly until it was opened by his mother, and then he rushed through and fell into her arms, exhausted.

For a moment Michael's mother didn't say anything, but looked out through the front door expecting to see John. When it was clear that he wasn't going to appear, she shut the door, called out to her husband, and turned to Michael again with a worried look on her face.

"Michael, tell me quickly, where is John, is he safe?"

For a few moments Michael just couldn't speak, he was so breathless, then he said: "Yes, he's all right, Mum. He's in a cottage some miles down the road." He gasped for breath again and then carried on: "He's looking after an old man and woman. I came to get some help because the old man is ill and he needs a doctor straight away."

Then Michael's father came up and spoke to him softly: "Where is the cottage, Michael, do you know?"

Michael nodded and pulled the envelope from his pocket and gave it to his father. "This is the address, Dad."

While Michael's mother put him to bed with

a hot drink and a hot water bottle, his father telephoned the police and told them all that had happened. A police car then drove a doctor to the cottage and later on that night brought John back home.

A police sergeant came into the house with John and asked if he could see Michael, to congratulate him on what he had done. So they all went upstairs and stood round Michael's bed.

"Well, young man," the police sergeant said to him, "the doctor only just got to the cottage on time. If it hadn't been for you the old man would probably have died, but now both he and his wife are safe in hospital. You're a very brave boy, you know. Not many adults would have braved that snowstorm as you did. Your brother, John, did a good job too, looking after the man and woman while you were gone. You have both proved yourselves to be very worthy Cub Scouts, and I should think that your Akela is going to be very proud of you, for I know that your mother and father certainly are."

A MARBLED PATTERN

Making a marbled pattern can be very enjoyable and is really quite easy. A marbled pattern is made by floating oil colours on the surface of water, and then transferring them on to a piece of paper. Oil colours mixed with turpentine can be used, and there is a ready-made colour which is prepared especially for these patterns. This is obtainable from artists' shops.

A shallow water-tight dish is needed about 20 inches × 10 inches, or an ordinary sink can be used. Artists' oil colours are mixed with turpentine and each colour is put into a small jar with a brush. Partly fill the dish with water and then drop a spot or two of each colour on to the surface of the water. These drops of oil colour will spread out over the surface—some colours spreading more easily than others. If any drops sink to the bottom of the dish then the colour is being put on too thickly.

Having put on a number of colours, draw a stick through the colours to give them movement, and to make a pattern. Patterns are varied according to strokes made with the stick.

When the pattern is ready take a piece of paper slightly smaller than the dish—an ordinary drawing paper is ideal. Lower one end of the paper on to the water and slowly lower the paper down on to the surface. The paper is then taken off immediately and the oil colours will have been transferred to the underside of the paper. The oil paint will be dry but the paper will be wet from the water and needs to be dried, by hanging up.

A great variety of patterns can be made in this way, and no two are exactly alike. When placing the paper on to the water do this slowly, otherwise air can get between the paper and the paint leaving an air gap and consequently a plain spot on the pattern.

Once dry, the patterns can be used for a great variety of things, such as: coverings for books, cardboard box coverings, photograph albums, address books, small notebooks and blotting pads.

Join the Adventure makers

Who are they?

They are the Scouts – with an action-packed programme that gives them the chance to make adventure.

How do you join?

If you are a $10\frac{1}{2}$ year old Cub Scout with a Link Badge then you have begun, so make sure you get into the Troop.

Here's what the 'Adventure Makers' do:

CAMPING

For a week or a weekend, with the whole Troop or just with your Patrol.

You'll be preparing your own site, your own fire and your own meals. Have you ever tried 'backwoodsman' cooking? You *could* do as an 'Adventure Maker'.

EXCITING PROGRAMME

Want to be an Airman, Boatman, Sportsman – like to pioneer and observe? Would you like to be a Craftsman, Forester, Explorer, Skin Diver or Archaeologist? All these badges can be gained as a Scout. Plus working for your Scout Standard and Advanced Scout Standard, and then the Chief Scout's Award.

NEW FRIENDS

A Scout is a Brother to every other Scout. Lots of new friends await you in the Troop.

NEW ACTIVITIES

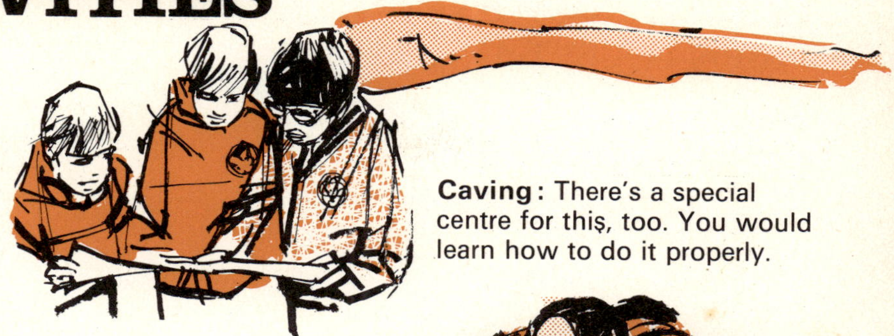

Hiking: With your Patrol or with a friend. Planning your own route, using map and compass.

Caving: There's a special centre for this, too. You would learn how to do it properly.

Boating: Sailing, Canoeing can all be done with the Scouts: there are special Activity Centres to teach you how.

Climbing: Lots of Scouts do this – so could you.

Folk Singing: Do you play an instrument or sing? Lots of Troops do folk singing. You could even end up at the National Folk-Fest.

Country-wide Wide Game: All the excitement of mysterious phone-calls, secret 'bombs' and lots more.

Gang Show: Lots of Scouts take part in these shows. All the glitter and excitement and, of course, the 'nerves' of a big show.

Scout Bands: Ever wanted to beat the big drum? Many Troops have Bands.

Activity Weeks: Many areas run special activity weeks for Scouts – lots of adventure there.

Special Camp Sites: There's many sites around the country you could visit with the 'Adventure Makers'.

Set sail for adventure abroad. See new places, discover how people *really* live abroad, camp in the sun. All can be done with the Scouts.

A host of adventures await you in the 'Adventure Makers'. Make sure you don't miss out. Happy Adventures!

Rearing Butterflies and Moths

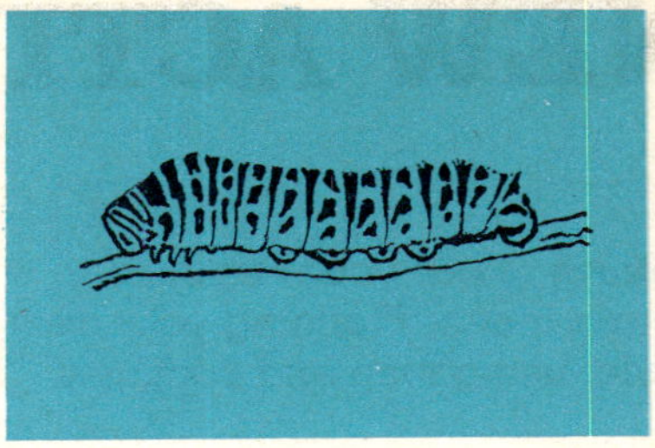

The caterpillar of the rare Swallowtail butterfly *(Papilio machaon)*, today mostly found only in the fens of Norfolk and Cambridgeshire, where it feeds on milk parsley, fennel, etc. (Actual size).

The handsome, remarkably hairy caterpillar of the Vapourer moth *(Orgyia antiqua)*. Feeds on the foliage of a wide variety of trees and bushes in summer. (Greatly enlarged).

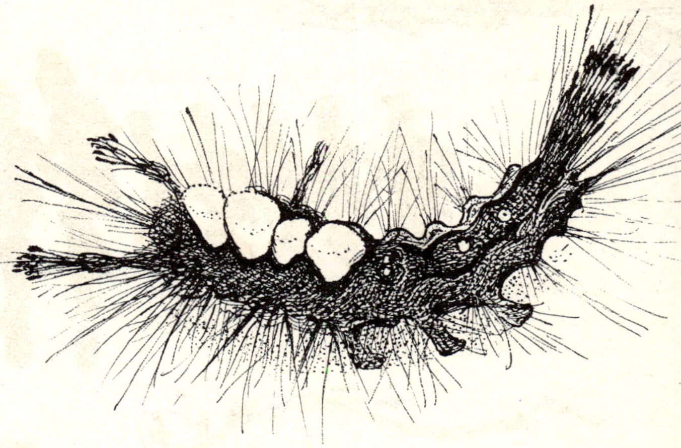

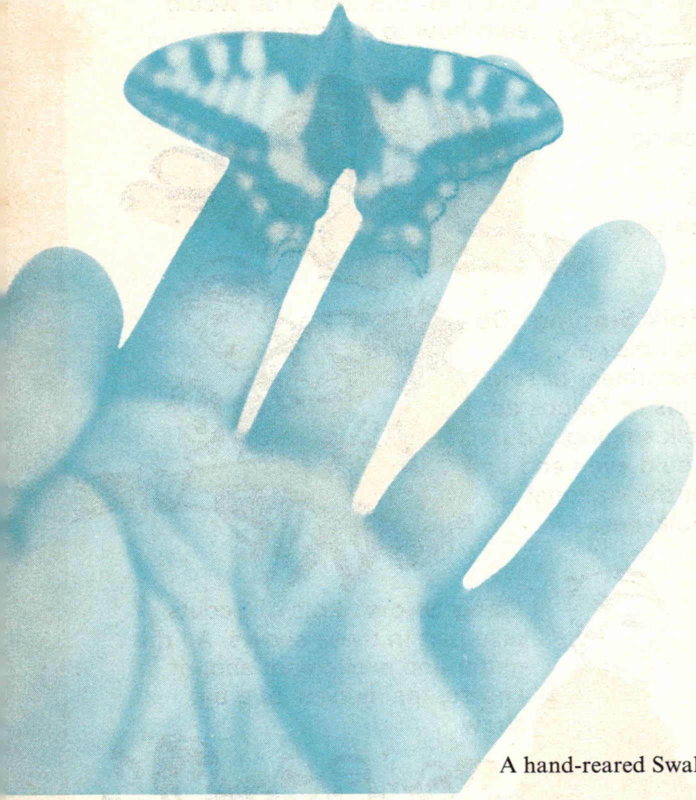

A hand-reared Swallowtail butterfly *(Papilio machaon)*.

If you are a collector of butterflies and moths – scientifically known as Lepidoptera, 'scale winged' insects – then it is worth remembering that there is much more to the hobby than simply capturing the adult insects in the field.

Breeding butterflies and moths from their eggs, caterpillars or chrysalides is far and away the best method of obtaining perfect specimens for your collection. The reasons for this are many and various. For one thing, butterflies and moths in the wild are liable to suffer damage to their wings after even a short period of activity – and there is nothing worse than a tattered specimen in the cabinet. In addition, both the winged adults and their early stages are in constant danger of being eaten by a variety of predatory animals, whereas if bred in captivity they have an optimum chance of survival. But there are also plenty of other good reasons.

I am not a collector myself, and my own object in breeding these insects is simply a means of studying in detail and at first hand the infinite variation between the individual life histories of the different species; there are 68 species of butterflies and over 2000 different kinds of larger moths in Britain. Unless there are special reasons for keeping them, I nearly always release the adult insects I have reared from their early stages, being perfectly satisfied with the information and interest I have gleaned in the process.

But that doesn't mean the collector cannot combine the two ideas; indeed, any collector must surely gain infinitely greater satisfaction from the possession of a set specimen which he has bred from egg, caterpillar or chrysalis, and of whose life history he has kept detailed notes, than one which he obtained simply by netting it as an adult insect – unless, of course, it was captured under particularly unusual, memorable or difficult circumstances.

Breeding most butterflies and moths is not too difficult and for much of the year, from early summer until well into autumn, the early stages may be looked for, with some expectation of success, in a great variety of places.

Practically every species of tree, bush or lowly plant has its own particular Lepidopteran enemy or enemies. Most caterpillars feed on leafage, but some, like those of the Swift moths, dwell in the ground,

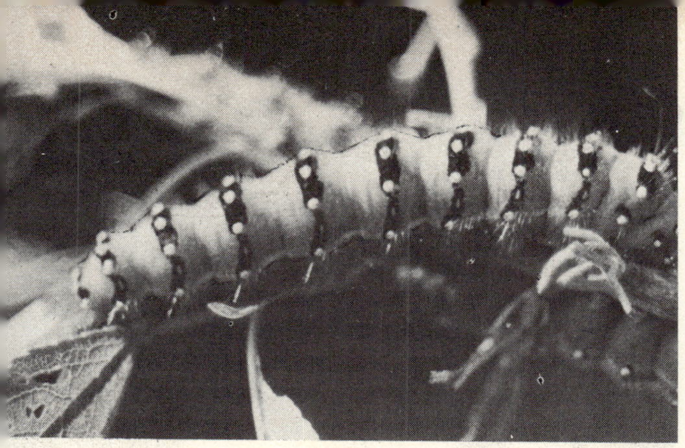

Caterpillar of Emperor moth *(Saturnia pavonia)*. Feeds on heather, bramble, sloe, etc. (Enlarged).

A typical mixed hedgerow with hawthorn, sloe, wild rose, blackberry, ash, etc.: excellent for caterpillars of various species.

feeding on the roots of plants, while others again – the Goat moth is an example – live in rotting wood.

COLLECTING CATERPILLARS

Possibly the best approach for the beginner intent on breeding butterflies and moths from livestock collected in the field is first to select a single promising-looking area and concentrate on seeing what that produces. In May and June, for example, thick mixed hedges are especially rewarding in producing a variety of caterpillar species. If these contain, as they generally do in the midlands and south, hawthorn, wild rose and sloe (blackthorn), then you are almost certain to discover at this time of the year larvae of common species like the Yellow-tail, Magpie and Vapourer moths.

The Yellow-tail caterpillar is an extremely striking creature with its bright red and black colouration, warty body and long greyish hairs. It feeds on all three of the food-plants I have just mentioned and is very easy to rear.

The Magpie larva is quite different in appearance, belonging to a large group, the caterpillars of which are generally known as 'loopers' from their characteristic mode of progressing by bending their bodies into a kind of loop. Unlike other groups, loopers have only two pairs of 'false' legs or pseudopodia – called false because they are lost in the change to adult insect – which are present as hind claspers and widely separated from the six true legs situated just behind the head. To move the whole of their bodies therefore these caterpillars have to raise their hind-quarters and slide them along the twig or leaf on which they are standing to meet the true legs, thus forming an upright loop shape.

Magpie larvae are rather thin, white in colour with orange and black markings. Like Yellow-tails, they eat sloe and hawthorn and are often so common as to constitute a pest in gardens, where they frequently eat the leafage of gooseberry and currant bushes.

Vapourer larvae, curiously enough, are nowhere so common as in urban parks, where they may be found on almost any kind of tree leafage. If you find *a young* Vapourer caterpillar you may well be puzzled to find that it does not seem to conform to the illustrations in guide books on the subject. This is because, in common with all caterpillars, they pass through several skin changes before they reach full-fed condition, ready for pupation, and each stage is markedly different in colouration.

At first the Vapourer larva is blackish in body colour, not very hairy but with long black and yellow tufts on its back. Then comes a transformation in which the characteristic 'toothbrush' hairs on the back become all pale yellow, and the body is covered with a uniform series of bright red dots. Finally we have the last-stage larva in all its hirsute splendour, and this is the stage most books illustrate.

The methods used to collect caterpillars in the field must obviously depend to a large extent on the type of habitat explored.

With hedges one can simply wander along slowly, just *looking* hard – and this, to my mind, is by far the best method, because it teaches the naturalist to use his eyes to the best advantage. Indeed, it is quite extraordinary what the entomologist can find in such places after a little practice, while the ordinary countryside stroller perhaps passes by oblivious of the wonders just under his nose.

Another, more energetic method is particularly applicable to searching trees, which it is not always convenient to ascend merely to look for caterpillars! This method involves spreading a large white cloth beneath the food plant and giving one of the branches a series of sharp shakes. This will usually result in a positive shower of small life, particularly with trees like oak, which are among the most persecuted of all vegetable growths. Much of the fall will be not at all what the lepidopterist is looking for: earwigs, tiny spiders, bugs, although each is of interest. Some species, like the larvae of hawk-moths, cling to their food-plant extremely tenaciously and thus are not easy to dislodge by shaking; but then they frequently make up for this by their size and the telltale inroads they make on the leafage of their choice. A little time spent looking up into the foliage of a low tree, or from beneath a bush like privet, will often prove rewarding in this respect, for the majority of caterpillars feed on the undersides of the leaves.

Sometimes, having obtained a caterpillar by the beating method from, say, a tangled hedge, one is not always sure exactly which plant it was feeding on. In this case, it is best to take a sample of each likely plant and note which the larva feeds on in captivity. Identification of larvae is a fascinating business and can be facilitated to some extent by reference to such books as W. J. Stokoe's *Caterpillars of the British Butterflies* and the companion two volumes on the *Caterpillars of the British Moths*.

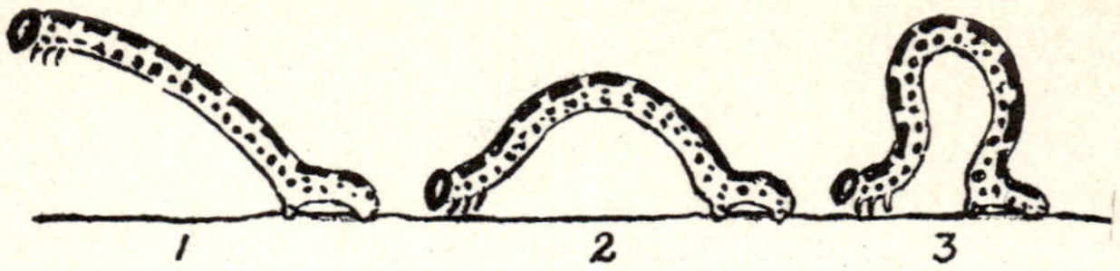

The caterpillar of the very common Magpie moth *(Abraxas grossulariata)*, showing the characteristic looping method of progress. Feeds on sloe and hawthorn in early summer. (Actual size).

The cocoon of a Puss moth and, inset, pupa removed from its cocoon. (Actual size).

WHAT THEY NEED

What provisions you make for the caterpillars in your care in the way of housing depends very much on the species. Most butterflies and many moths pupate or turn into chrysalides against the stems of the food plant or at the bottom of it, so that, in essentials, all that is required is a plentiful and continuous supply of fresh food.

Others, like those of the hawk-moths, burrow into the ground for several inches where they make a large cocoon and pupate inside it. In such cases, it is best to provide a basal mixture of peat and sandy soil which, being much less likely to dry into a hard solid mass, is easier for the caterpillar to tunnel into and for the emerging moth to negotiate. Often, however, it is safer to disinter the pupae, after a decent interval to ensure that the pupal change *has* taken place, subsequently placing them in airtight tins until near the time of emergence.

Pupae – and this also applies to very young caterpillars – require very little air, and enclosed in airtight containers they are safe from the attacks of parasitic flies, 'micro' moths and other tiny creatures that wage a constant war against the larvae and pupae of butterflies and the larger moths. Inside the tin the humidity level will remain relatively stable and thus prevent any chance of the pupa drying up.

But do remember to take the pupae out once winter is well over: place them on dry moss or cotton wool and arrange a few pieces of twig or bark nearby for the emerging moth to climb and hang from while drying its wings.

It is also possible, of course, to take the shortest cut to obtaining perfect insects in captivity by collecting your pupae in the field. Very few of our butterflies over-winter as chrysalides, so that one has some chance of finding them throughout the summer months wherever their food plant abounds. The vast majority of British moths, however, pass the long period from about September to May as pupae, perhaps in the soil, beneath the bark of trees, or attached to the outside of them (the hard cocoons of the Puss moth, for example).

Searching for pupae is an exciting occupation for the autumn and winter months. Obtaining one's pupae in this way has the added fascination in that sometimes it is almost impossible to determine the species, so that you just don't know what you've got until the moth emerges!

SEARCHING FOR EGGS

If searching for caterpillars and pupae is a somewhat uncertain business, then what can be said for one's chances of finding the eggs of butterflies and moths! These are usually very tiny and inconspicuous; often they are tucked away under leaves, quite commonly one egg to a leaf!

It is difficult to induce butterflies to mate in captivity and thus obtain eggs that way, because they usually require lots of space and this is generally beyond the

A line of willow trees which can be examined for the eggs, larvae and pupae (cocoons) of the Puss moth *(Cerura vinula)* in summer.

A newly-emerged Puss moth. (Greatly enlarged).

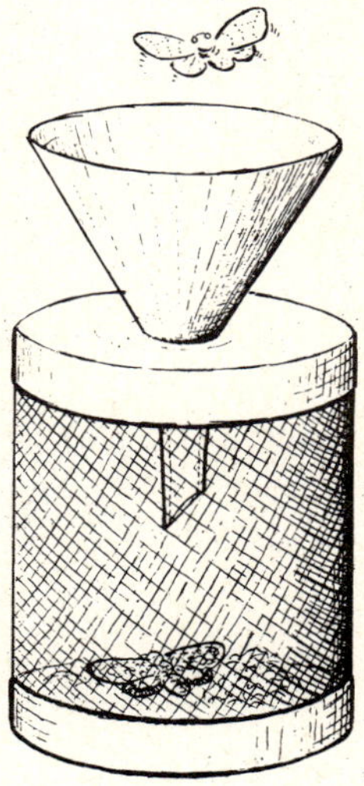

An 'assembling' cage with sides of gauze or muslin and funnel opening. The aperture can be stopped as soon as one or more male moths have entered the cage.

average enthusiast. With moths, however, it is often possible to obtain eggs by the method known as assembling. A freshly emerged female moth is placed out of doors in a container having a funnel-shaped aperture, allowing access to male moths, who are attracted by the lady's particular scent, but largely preventing the insects' escape. Once inside the male or males will probably be disinclined to leave anyway! Subsequent to mating, the female will usually oblige by depositing eggs in such containers as you provide for her. Eggs vary in the time they take to hatch; but the nearness to this happening is usually indicated by the fact that they darken, often almost to black, just before the tiny larvae emerge. Make sure that fresh young leafage is immediately available for the youngsters.

KEEP YOUR NOTES

Obviously, to get the very best out of keeping insects like butterflies and moths one should make careful and detailed notes of everything that happens from the very beginning. Dates of collection, food-plant(s), initial size and colouration of caterpillar, pupa or eggs, where found – all should be recorded. Subsequently, dates and, if possible, times of a caterpillar's skin changes, pupation, and finally emergence of the perfect insect may be added.

In the end, if you feel you must keep the adult insect, you have its complete personal 'dossier' too, which adds tremendously to its value scientifically.

Many of our moths' and butterflies' habits and the appearance of the different larval instars – as the stages between skin changes are called – are little known, and carefully kept records are always of interest, not least to other entomologists or collectors. In addition, in keeping and rearing insects it is often possible to be present when unusual happenings or critical stages in an insect's life history take place – making wonderful subjects for a descriptive pen.

I vividly remember some years ago keeping a caterpillar of an Eyed hawk-moth in a glass container, the bottom of which was filled with earth. To my joy, the full fed larva tunnelled down and obligingly made its cocoon right against the side of the glass, thus affording me a grandstand view of the whole process of change to pupa: the splitting of the larval skin and the gradual emergence of the chrysalis, which at first was a beautiful shade of bright green but which gradually darkened to rich brown and then almost to black.

It is possible that you may eventually wish to write up and publish your observations in some form or another. No, this *isn't* beyond you! There is a journal which is specifically designed for the young amateur insect enthusiast to record his observations. It is the *Bulletin* of the Amateur Entomologists' Society, the address of which can be obtained through any public library. Through the medium of such a journal, enthusiasts all over the country, and overseas, are able to exchange views and observations to their mutual profit and interest. I would strongly recommend any young entomologist to join this society.

Naturally in a short article like this I have only been able to skim the surface of the subject of breeding Lepidoptera. Each species presents its own particular fascination and perhaps problems. The book on butterfly caterpillars I mentioned earlier includes an excellent chapter on methods of rearing eggs, larvae and pupae in captivity. There are also two special volumes on the subject, both of which are produced by the same publishing house, Warne. These are: Brian Worthington-Stuart's *Collecting and Breeding Butterflies and Moths* and R. L. E. Ford's *Practical Entomology*.

Now it only remains for me to wish you: Good hunting and good rearing!

*ALL ILLUSTRATIONS by ANTHONY WOOTTON

THE HARDY URCHIN

SOME years ago, in early autumn, a neighbour of mine was forking over a rubbish heap in his garden when he found three tiny baby hedgehogs at the bottom. They were quite blind, motionless save for a feeble wriggling, and their flesh was soft, wrinkled and pink. I remember that our friend carefully transferred them to a nearby hedge bank, hoping that the mother, or sow, hedgehog would find the little creatures—for young urchins are totally dependent on their mother until about two months old, when they begin to forage for food on their own account.

Whether or not hedgehogs are scarcer today than they were is not altogether easy to say. Perhaps it is simply that the animals' secretive, largely nocturnal habits mislead us into *thinking* along these lines. Admittedly, a good many wandering hedgehogs meet an untimely death on our increasingly busy roads, due in part to their instinctive habit of rolling up into a ball at the approach of danger.

But these attractive little mammals are still fairly common in much of our countryside, even in the suburbs of towns. At a camp site or in a fair-sized garden, particularly one bounded by a thick hedge and near open country, we can often attract a hedgehog simply by putting out a saucer of milk at night, because all hedgehogs love milk, and will sometimes go to great lengths to get it.

Not long ago, a hedgehog was observed to be making off with a milk carton clamped over its head, the householder's sleep having been disturbed by the animal's blind noisy scufflings! Doubtless it had been after the few drops of milk left in the bottom. There is even a belief that hedgehogs sometimes take sips from the udders of reclining cows, though it is difficult to say how much truth there is in the idea.

For the greater part of the year, however, hedgehogs have no need to indulge in petty theft, because they can usually find all they require in the way of natural food with the minimum of effort. Indeed they are among our most useful pest controllers. They are especially fond of slugs and snails—which is why they are often so active on rainy evenings, when the wet conditions bring these molluscs out from their lairs. 'Prickles' will also eat cockroaches, beetles, and a wide variety of other invertebrate animals, while even small rodents like mice, rats and voles are sometimes taken. The hedgehog is, too, an implacable enemy of reptiles, notably the adder or viper, to the poison of which it is said—probably wrongly—to be immune.

Apart from man—who still kills them for various reasons—hedgehogs have relatively few enemies. Gamekeepers sometimes accuse them of taking game-birds' eggs, probably with small reason, and gypsies have a high regard for their meat, baking them in a covering of clay.

Certain carnivores, like badgers and foxes, have devised methods of making the prickly fellow unroll—the fox with a rather unorthodox method; but if it chooses to 'stay indoors', it is hard to think of any British animal which could do much about it.

Even to pick a hedgehog up is, as anyone who has tried it will know, something of an endurance test. Its spines are arranged in such a complicated, multi-

directional way that gloves seem the only answer to the problem. Just as in porcupines, to which the hedgehog is in no way related, the spines are really modified *hairs* which have developed a special protective quality. Young urchins have fewer hairs than the adults; these are soft and flexible, white at the outset, but later shed and replaced by a more numerous, stronger set.

Ancient writers tell us that the hedgehog's spines had other uses apart from protection, one of them being as a means of spearing and carrying apples back to its lair. Indeed there is a delightful illustration of hedgehogs doing just that in the 12th century Rochester Bestiary manuscript, preserved in the British Museum. Unfortunately for lovers of such appealing legends, the belief is now largely discredited, though there is no doubt that certain kinds of vegetable matter *are* included in the hedgehog's bill of fare.

Some of the common names for the hedgehog—such as hedge pig and boar and sow (for the male and female)—are not altogether inappropriate, incidentally. It has no real relation to pigs, of course, but its nose is large and pig-like, well adapted to rooting, while the animal's characteristic odour is certainly reminiscent of the sty! Like pigs, too, hedgehogs can be extraordinarily vocal at times. I remember once being startled to hear what sounded almost exactly like an owl hooting plaintively from the dense undergrowth below a low wall. I didn't catch sight of the animal, because it was dark, but the heavy rustling and piggy smell left me in no doubt as to the voice's owner. Grunts, squeaks, and even quite piercing screams—the last uttered especially when in danger—are also included in the hedgehog's vocal range, though normally it is a fairly silent beast, which is what we would expect from a creature of the night.

Urchin, the original Old English name for the hedgehog, derives from the Old French *Herichon,* this in turn from the Latin *Erinaceus*—the latter now forming part of its scientific name, *Erinaceus europaeus.* Nowadays, urchin is perhaps more often applied to dirty, rather mischievous little boys—not Cub Scouts, of course!—which some might consider a bit of a slight on the hedgehog, even accounting for the fleas which they almost invariably possess (the hedgehogs that is, not the boys!).

Although hedgehogs hibernate during the winter, usually from about November to April, they are rather uneven sleepers, and a mild spell will often awaken them into foraging for a meal. Sometimes they can be seen out and about even in the depths of the harshest winter. A man once went outside his house to investigate an overflow pipe which had burst. Under the cascading water, shaking itself vigorously and obviously enjoying its spartan bath immensely, was a hedgehog. The temperature at the time was six degrees below, and there was more than a foot of snow on the ground.

Somehow, urchin seems a bit of a misnomer after that!

THE escapologist

"I say, you two, come over here and take a look at this," Owen Waters said excitedly to his two Scout Troop pals, Freddie Barlow and Colin Prosser, as they walked down the main street of Mantonleigh, the small market town where they all lived.

"What on earth is going on?" Freddie asked quizzically, as he wiped the lenses of his spectacles with his handkerchief.

"It's one of those busker chaps who earn a living by entertaining passersby in the streets," Owen replied.

"Come on, let's take a closer look," Colin suggested, elbowing his way into the crowd.

"Can you see what he's doing?" Freddie asked.

"Yes, he's having several heavy chains bound tightly around him, and . . ."

"And what?" Colin interrupted.

"And they're being padlocked now," Owen continued.

"Now he's getting into a thick sack," Freddie announced as soon as he reached a convenient vantage point.

Suddenly the high-pitched voice of the escapologist's blonde female assistant rang out clearly over the noise of the dense crowd which had gathered to witness the amazing spectacle.

"Ladies and Gentlemen. You have all seen in front of you with your own eyes, the chains and locks which some of you have kindly bound around my partner. He will now get into the sack and the top will be securely fastened. He will then try to make his miraculous escape in less than a minute. If he doesn't, the oil-soaked sack will burst into flames when it is ignited by this flaming torch."

"Do you think he'll manage it?" Owen asked.

"I don't think he will in the time he's allowed, but I do know one thing though," Colin said.

"And what's that?" Freddie asked.

"I know I wouldn't like to risk it!" Colin said.

"Neither would I," Owen agreed.

"Oh! What's that?" Someone cried suddenly as there came a loud crash of breaking glass.

In the excitement of the moment the escapologist was forgotten as everyone realised that a smash and grab raid had taken place behind their unsuspecting backs.

"Quick, you two, down here!" Freddie commanded.

"Be sure to get the car number," Owen said as the three boys got themselves out from among the crowd and ran as fast as they could down a steep narrow cobbled alleyway.

"They'll have to come this way," Colin said excitedly.

"Yes. Yes, here they come!" Freddie said.

"All right, I'm ready," Owen said, as he produced a notebook from his breast pocket.

"Colour: blue," Freddie said.

"Make: Jaguar," Colin stated.

"And the number is. . ."

"EVY 972 D," Colin interrupted.

"Right, got it!" Owen said, clutching the book.

"Did either of you catch a glimpse of the occupants?" Colin asked.

"I only saw that there were two, and that they had stocking hood masks on," Freddie said, as the car sped on down the street, its tyres screeching as it disappeared round a sharp bend.

"Golly! They were lucky not to have met anyone. It's a busy time of the day," Colin gasped.

"Stand back. Here come the police," Owen said. Almost as soon as he had spoken, three police cars rushed by, their sirens blaring and their blue lights flashing.

The next day, the three pals were on their way home from a Scout Troop meeting which they had held to make some arrangements for their annual concert at the local old people's hospital.

"I thought that this shop was empty and waiting to be demolished," Owen said, as the boys came to some disused premises.

"So it is. Why do you ask?" Freddie queried.

"There's a faint light showing through from one of the back rooms, surely," Owen replied.

"You're seeing things again," Colin laughed.

"No I'm not. Just you wait a minute and it'll appear again," Owen said brusquely.

"Yes, there it is, it's back again," Colin stated emphatically.

"Shall we take a look?" Freddie suggested.

"You can never tell what may be going on in there," Owen said.

"I don't suppose we can get in," Colin reasoned.

"They got in, didn't they?" Owen asked forcefully.

"Yes, of course," Freddie agreed.

"Well then, why can't we?"

"I just happen to know a way in, which is through the garages, but we shall have to be very quiet," Colin said.

"All right, lead on," Owen agreed.

The boys retraced their steps to the street, turned into a dark passageway and eventually came to some large green doors, which formed the entrance to the garages.

"Blow! They're locked," Colin exclaimed impatiently as he tried to open them.

"Never mind. Perhaps there's another way?"

"Yes, as far as I can remember there is another door, further along the alley," Colin said.

"Let's take a look at it," Owen suggested.

"All right. It's open," Colin said excitedly as he reached it and lifted the latch.

"These stairs lead to a small storeroom at the back of the shop."

"How do you know all this?" Freddie asked.

"I used to deliver newspapers from this shop, every Saturday morning, until they closed down. Don't you remember?" Colin asked.

"Yes. Of course you did. I was forgetting that," Freddie agreed.

The boys made their way cautiously up the steep flight of ricketty stairs until they came to another door.

"This one is open, too," Freddie whispered.

"Look, more stairs!" Owen said as he peeped round it.

"I wonder?" Freddie mused.

"Yes?" Colin queried.

"I wonder if it leads down to the garages, that's all," Freddie continued.

"Yes, I think it does," Colin said.

"You don't think that . . ." Owen interjected.

"I'm not thinking anything at the moment. I'm just going to take a look. You two wait here," Freddie commanded.

He left his two pals and began to descend the stairs to the garages.

"There's only a car there," he laughed, when he returned to them a few minutes later.

"Then it's not important," Colin said.

"Wait a minute," Freddie said importantly.

"It just happens to be a blue Jaguar; and its number is EVY 972 D?" Owen guessed.

"That's right," Freddie said

"No! I don't believe it!" Colin gasped.

"It's perfectly true. If you don't believe me go and have a look for yourself," Freddie said.

Gold Arrow Awards: Neil Cochran, Ian Taylor and Michael Kendal of the 15th Barrow-in-Furness (St. Luke's) Cub Scout Pack, and Jonathon Lomas of the 2nd Peterlee (St. Cuthbert's C. of E.), Durham, Pack, are amongst the many Cub Scouts who gained their awards this year and got their names into the newspapers. Jonathon was the youngest holder of the award in Peterlee.

"I believe you now," Colin said.

"Now we shall have to be very quiet or they'll hear us," Freddie said.

"If they're still here," Owen said.

"Listen a minute. Can't you hear voices?" Colin said.

"I can now," Freddie agreed.

"And there are some bright lights as well," Owen put in.

"Hey! I'm going to take a peep through this chink in the woodwork," Freddie said.

"Can you see anyone?" Owen asked, just as soon as his pal had got his eye opposite the hole.

"Yes, there are four people in the next room," Freddie whispered his reply.

"Let me have a look," Colin pleaded.

"Not for a minute. I bet you'll never guess who is in there," Freddie said placing his hand over the hole.

"Oh! Come on, tell us," Colin said.

"Yes, come on. Who are they?" Owen pleaded.

"They're . . ." Freddie started.

"I dont' believe it. They're the escape artist,

his assistant and two other men!" Colin exclaimed as he peeped cautiously into the storeroom.

"Keep quiet! Try to hear what they're talking about," Freddie suggested.

"Shush. I'm not sure, but it sounds as if they're planning another jeweller's shop raid," Colin said.

"Where?" Freddie asked enthusiastically.

"Right here," Colin said.

"Here in Mantonleigh?" Freddie questioned.

"Why yes. The busker has just said that he thought that it would have been much easier if it had been Barber-Thompsons in Church Street," Colin told them.

"Anything else?" Owen asked.

"One of the thieves, a big man, I suppose he must have been the car driver, said that he agreed, but they'll have to try it one day next week, probably Wednesday."

"Golly!" Freddie exclaimed.

"What shall we do?"

"The first thing to do is to get safely out of here. If they should hear us now, there's no knowing what they'd do to us," Colin said nervously.

"All right, then. Come on. Don't make any noise," Freddie said.

"We'll have to tell the police immediately, then they can come and arrest them," Owen said.

"Good idea. Right. Lead on to the police station," Colin agreed.

The boys crept noiselessly out into the alleyway and then hurried along the street to the police station, where they related their story to the constable on duty. They were most surprised when he thanked them for their information and the trouble they had taken, and then invited them to go with him for a ride around Mantonleigh in a police car on the next Wednesday.

The next few days seemed an age to the three boys, who were excited at the prospect of having a ride in a police car. But they were puzzled because as far as they knew no arrest of the thieves had been made. However, on Wednesday, at the appointed time, they presented themselves at the police station.

"Hello, boys. I thought you'd soon be here. Come on, get in," the constable said, as he and the three boys piled into the waiting vehicle. The constable drove at a steady pace through the town and stopped almost outside Barber-Thompson's, the jewellers.

"What's going on here?" Owen asked.

"The busker is talking to that policeman," Freddie exclaimed.

"If you look very carefully I think you'll spot the other thieves among the people over there," the constable said, indicating a van which was dispensing cups of hot coffee and sandwiches.

"Yes. There's the blonde assistant," Colin said excitedly.

"And what are all those vans and that pile of electrical equipment doing?" Owen asked.

"I was hoping you'd soon notice that," the constable laughed.

"I can't see the joke," Freddie said impatiently.

"Well, boys, I'll tell you. This is a film unit on location. The smash and grab raid which you witnessed last week was a kind of trial run, if you like to call it that," the policeman explained.

"What about the newsagent's shop then?" Colin asked.

"And the conversation we overheard?" Owen put in.

"The conversation you overheard was a few of the cast trying to decide on a hide-out and which jeweller's shop would be the best one to feature in the film."

"I see," Freddie said, a note of disappointment in his voice. "And I thought that we were on to something really exciting."

"Never mind. Come on, get out and meet some of the cast. I'm sure you'll recognise one or two. And by the way, there'll be free tickets for you when the film comes to the local cinema. A reward for you all from the station sergeant. He was very pleased that you all took the trouble to come in and to report the conversation which you overheard. It might have been the real thing."

sports & pastimes

CLUES ACROSS.

1. Game with each team numbering 15 players.
3. Famous race course in Surrey.
6. Series of races in which yachts take part.
8. Long wooden runner strapped to foot for moving over snow.
9. To contend as teams on opposite sides.
10. Kind of jump usually in Show Jumping courses.
11. Long tapering stick used in Billiards.
12. A referee might well send you ---.
16. Some players might have this kind of match.
17. Penalties are these.
18. Game of Eastern origin played on a board of 64 squares.

CLUES DOWN.

1. The Oaks and The Derby are just two.
2. These occur in Cricket.
4. Place of maintenance at car-racing venues.
5. The ------ Carlo Rally.
7. Race Course near Liverpool.
11. Substance sometimes put on the end of a Billiard cue.
13. Eton ------ was first recorded in 1825.
14. A kind of 'Lift' in weight lifting.
15. A kind of jump in Athletics.

ANSWERS

ACROSS

1. RUGBY. 3. EPSOM. 6. REGATTA. 8. SKI. 9. VIE. 10. WATER. 11. CUE. 12. OFF. 16. BENEFIT. 17. KICKS. 18. CHESS.

DOWN

1. RACES. 2. BYES. 4. PITS. 5. MONTE. 7. AINTREE. 11. CHALK. 13. FIVES. 14. JERK. 15. HIGH.

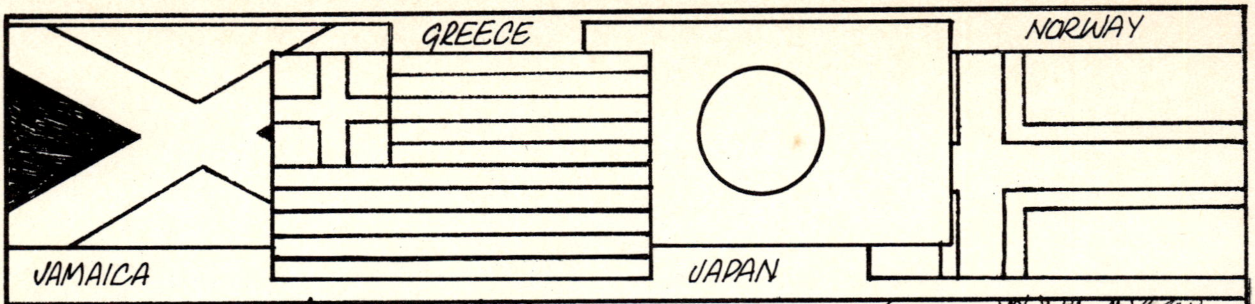
GREECE
NORWAY
JAMAICA
JAPAN

PETER HARRISON.

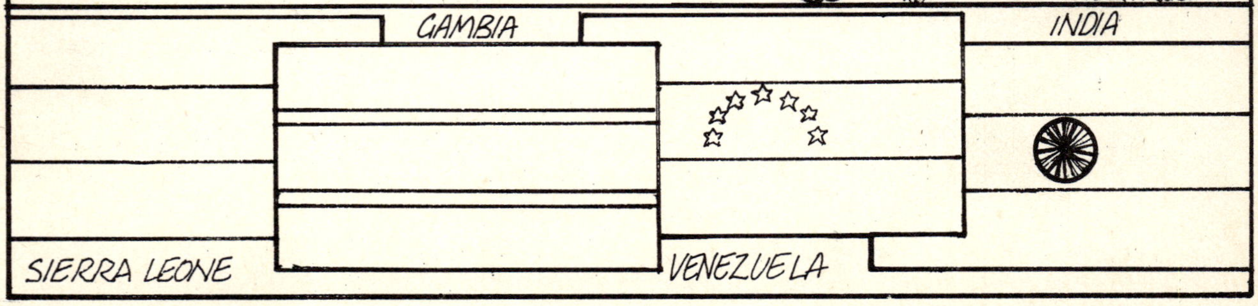
GAMBIA
INDIA
SIERRA LEONE
VENEZUELA

COLOURING COMPETITION

On the opposite page is a picture, drawn by our artist, and, which you can colour with paint, crayon or felt tip pen. Then, when you have done this to your satisfaction, you must colour the flags of the countries named in their correct colours. You will find all these in *The Observer's Book of Flags.* Then you must remove the page from your Annual and send it to The Editor, The Cub Scout Annual, 25 Buckingham Palace Road, London SW1W 0PY, to arrive not later than 28th February 1974. Prizes will be awarded as follows and the Editor's decision is final:

1st Prize: Book or record token to the value of £10.
2nd Prize: Books to the value of £2·50.
3rd Prize: Books to the value of £1·50.
10 Consolation Prizes of a book each.

the lonely TRAIL

I camped last night in a glade by a brook
  Where the wind whispered soft in the trees.
I built my fire and I cooked me a meal,
  And I sat like a king at my ease.

I looked below where the brook hurried by
  With a song and a laugh just for me.
I looked above at the trees all athrill
  With the joy of a life full and free.

I looked again and I saw the blue sky,
  And the gleam of the sun in the west,
And the peace of the evening enfolded me,
  And I slept like a bird in its nest.

W. K. Watts

ALL THE FUN OF THE FAIR

Everybody enjoys a Country Fair, and if you are planning to have Visitors' Day at your next Pack Holiday, or a garden fête for Group Funds, or just an ordinary Parents' Night in the Pack Den, you could hardly do better than to include one in the programme.

This will provide you with three-way fun. To begin with there is the fun of inventing, making, and setting up your sideshows; then there's the fun of trying them out yourselves, and lastly there's the fun of acting as barkers at your fair—"Roll up! Roll up! Three free shots for fathers! Mums half-price!"—and watching the grown-ups having a bash.

The ideas in the chart are just to get you going. No doubt, once you start talking it over among yourselves other ideas will occur to you—coconut shies with empty coffee tins and conkers or bean bags; ball-in-the-bucket, with the bucket swinging like a pendulum from an overhead beam or branch; horizontal darts with the target marked out with sisal and metal skewers on the ground, and darts made by driving three-inch nails through noggins of wood, and so on. Half the fun comes in making use of odds and ends of equipment and material—empty tins, squeezy bottles, cotton reels, plywood tea chests, orange boxes, garden canes, rubber bands, and whatever else you can find. Indeed, the odds and ends themselves will often give you the idea for the sideshow—for instance, the Guided Parachute in the chart was obviously inspired when the artist felt the puff of an empty squeezy bottle on his face as he squeezed it!

If you decide to run your sideshows on the lines of a Country Fair it will add to the excitement if you have 'stage money' prizes with a special award of some sort for the winning competitor. You could have fun preparing the 'award', too! See what you can do by making a mulch of shredded egg-box and water with a tablespoonful of polyfilla mixed in, and then modelling a presentation cup, which can later be painted with silver. Or you could build up a splendid trophy by sellotaping four empty squeezy bottles together, three at the top and one forming the stem (remember to weight it with sand for stability) and graceful (plastic) handles fitted to the sides.

I hope you will find the illustrations in the chart fairly easy to follow. In SWAT THAT RAT a tennis ball is rolled down a sloping tube and is swatted as it shoots out of the bottom end. Half a dozen empty tins of the same size sellotaped together, with canes secured with rubber-bands at each side, will give you an excellent tube, and a short stick is all you will need for the swatter.

WILLIAM TELL is a circle of light plywood with William's face drawn with coloured chalk on the front and a cocoa tin stuck on the reverse side with sellotape. William is mounted in a frame in such a fashion that when his apple is struck fair and square with the arrow he does a sort of cartwheel and spills a number of marbles out of the tin. The number of marbles can be changed each time by the barker in charge of the sideshow, so that a competitor never knows how much he is going to win until William does his cartwheel.

A good way to mount your plywood William in the frame is to shave one side of each of two cotton reels to give you a flat surface which can then be glued to the back of the plywood near the sides. Six-inch nails driven through the framework will make highly efficient spindles, and if necessary extra cotton reels can be fitted to act as bearings or distance-pieces.

The shooting mechanism consists of two strings of rubber bands linked with larkshead knots, with a strip of rubber between them to hold the arrow, which is merely a light garden cane with the butt-end weighted, and protected, with more rubber bands.

Every Cub Scout is familiar with the Aerial Runway but here we have something called the AERIAL GUNWAY! As you see, the idea is that one end of the 'gunway' (just a long length of thin cord) is secured to a tree or other fixed object while the other is tied to a garden cane which is held by one of the competitors. The line runs through a pyramid of empty tins, and the object of the exercise is to shoot the 'missile' (a cotton reel) along the 'gunway' so that it passes through the pyramid without upsetting the tins and strikes the cane at the far end. The firing mechanism is another cotton reel with two strings of rubber bands sellotaped to the sides. Our experience is that this sideshow is always very popular with fathers, and it will add to the interest if you make it a Father-and-Son event, with one of them holding the cane and the other firing the missile.

In GUIDED PARACHUTES, light paper cones are threaded on to parallel strings stretched tightly between two posts, and are blown along by puffs from empty squeezy bottles. As a variation, you might like to set the two competitors off simultaneously from opposite ends of the same line. The first to reach the middle—marked with a cardboard disc—wins the prize.

CHOPSTICK CHAMPIONS is a simple relay in which empty tins are picked up with chopsticks at one end of the course and deposited on canes stuck in the ground at the other. The chopsticks are simply four-foot garden canes bound with rubber bands about twelve inches from one end, with another rubber band stretched across the tips.

All these ideas, of course, have been tested in our own field laboratory and have been given the CUB SCOUT ANNUAL seal of approval. It cannot be over-emphasised, however, that in matters of this sort *your own ideas are the best*. By all means make use of some of the suggestions in this article for your next Country Fair, but do, *do*, DO invent some of your own.

kite kapers

1

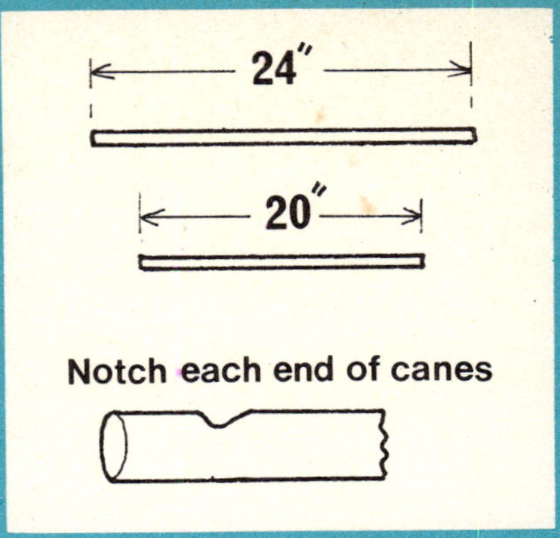

2

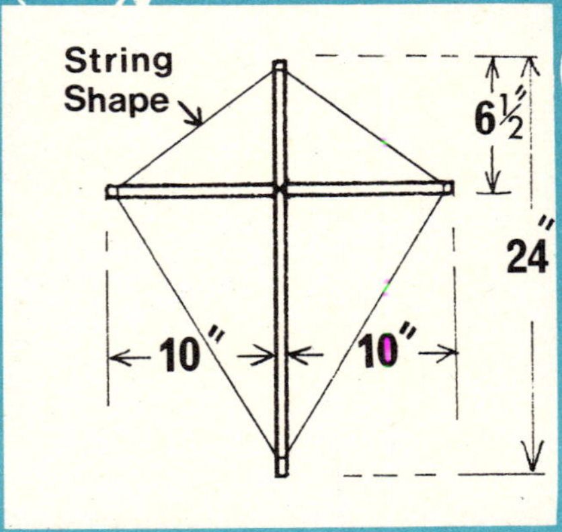

When you have decided the type of kite you wish to make, select your materials. The canes should be as light as possible, small pea canes used by Dad in the garden are suitable, but dowelling ⅛″ diameter will be much straighter and make it easier to get the final shape right.

(a) Cut the canes or dowelling to the required lengths. Slightly notch both ends of each cane with a knife or saw, as shown in Fig. 1. This will help to keep the string in place when making the kite shape.

(b) Lay canes in position, checking the dimensions with a ruler. Make sure that the cross stick is the same length on each side of centre cane (see Fig. 2).

(c) Tie the sticks together, making certain that the shape has an even appearance.

(d) Tie fine string to the notch at the top of the centre cane, then tie to the notches on each cane in turn, finishing up at the first knot. This gives the kite shape shown in Fig. 2.

3

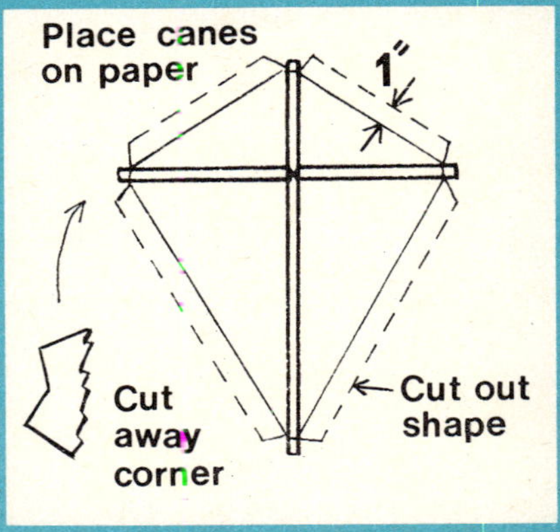

A PAPER DART

1

2

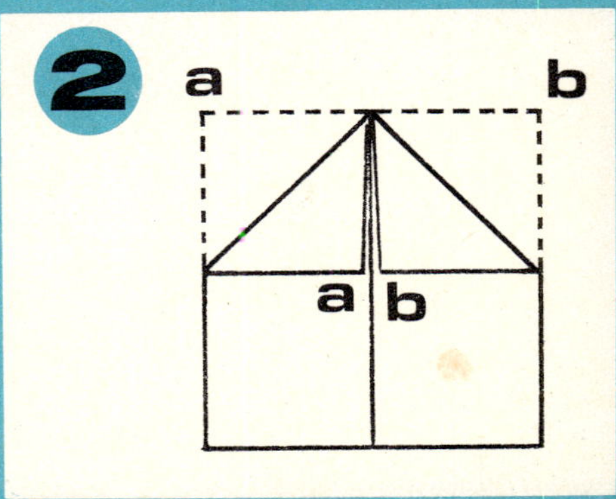

(a) Fold a sheet of paper in half (Fig. 1). Then open paper out flat.

(b) Fold a to a_1
Fold b to b_1
(Fig. 2)

4

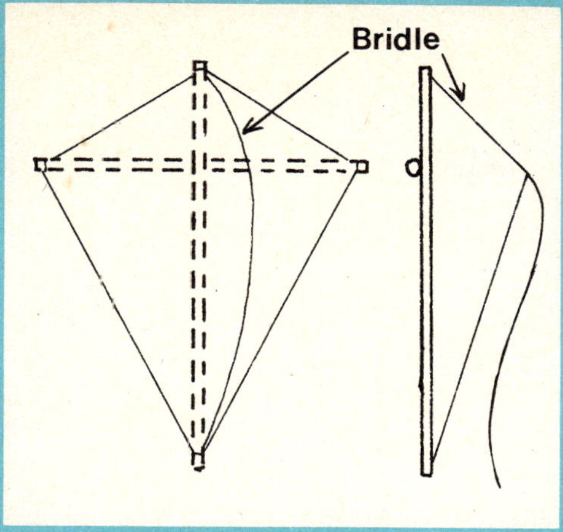

5

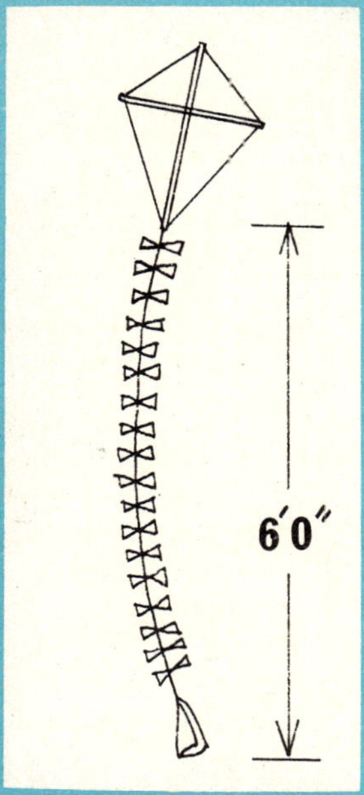

6

(e) Now for the covering, this can be tissue paper, brown paper, or polythene sheet. Place the canes on the paper, and draw lines about 1″ away from the string, cutting away the corners where canes occur and along drawn lines. See Fig. 3.

(f) Fold the margins of the paper over the string. Open up folds, glue margins, and then fold back over the string. Allow time for the glue to dry.

(g) Turn the kite over, so that the canes are behind the paper. Tie a length of string to the top of the centre cane, then to the bottom of the cane to form bridle – Fig. 4.

(h) Attach a 6′ 0″ length of string to the bottom of the kite; roll pieces of paper (about 6″) into a bow, and tie these to the tail string at about every 6″ (knot shown in Fig. 6). A piece of cloth (handkerchief size) is then tied to the end of the tail – Fig. 5. (This helps to keep the tail straight when flying.)

(i) Finally attach the flying string to the bridle with a slip knot. This will allow adjustments to the towing point.

HINTS ON FLYING

Kites can be flown in most open areas, such as a park, but do keep away from buildings and trees, as the air currents will cause the kite to dart.

Only fly your kite when there is some wind, as no kite will fly on a calm day.

If your kite does not fly at first, try adjusting the towing point on the bridle. If the towing point is too high, the kite will lie flat, and if it is too low it will become top heavy.

When flying the kite, stand with your back to the wind, and when you feel the wind pulling, let the kite into the air and let out the towing string.

Once the kite has made some height it can be made to climb by letting out some string, and then giving gentle pulls.

Finally, take care when bringing the kite down. Wind it in slowly and if the pull becomes too great let some string out, only winding again when the pull decreases.

3

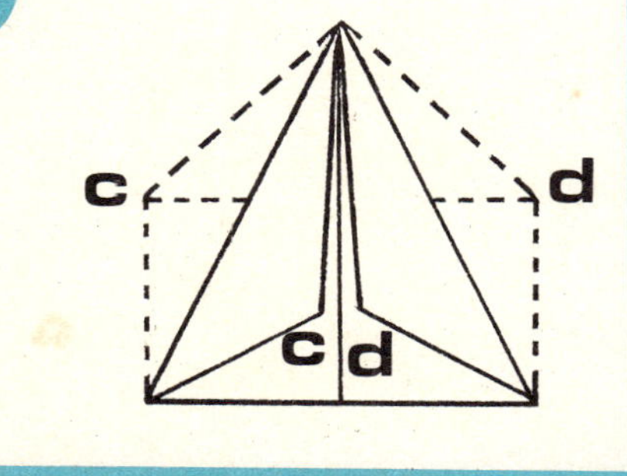

(c) Fold c to c_1
Fold d to d_1
(Fig. 3)

4

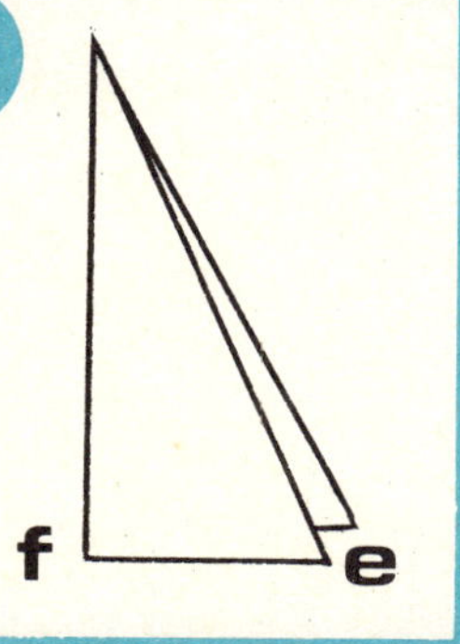

(d) Fold in half (Fig. 4).
Fold e to f
repeat on other side.

5

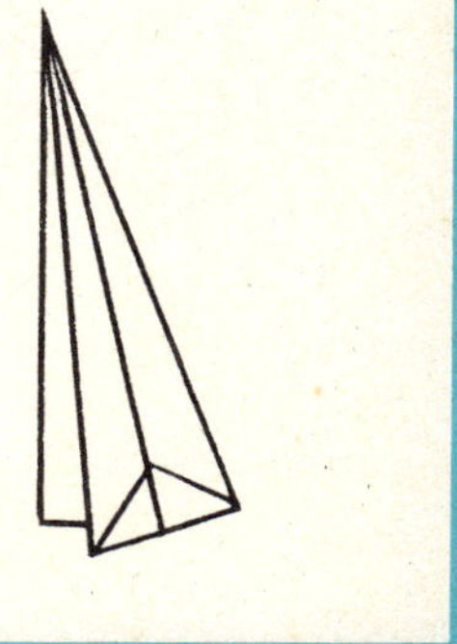

(e) Open flaps to make Fig. 5.

The hunt in Humblie's Wood

The distant growling throb of powerful motor-cycle engines beat through the hot August afternoon air as Alex and his Patrol, the Eagles, headed along the dusty country road to their camp in Humblie's Wood. The Scouts had finished a successful morning's orienteering practice in the valley.

"Gosh, I'm starved!" exclaimed Mike who, though the shortest Scout in the Patrol, had the makings of a good Sumo wrestler.

"Good grief!" said Barry, the A.P.L., "how can you be hungry, Mike? You ate most of the sandwiches! And the chocolate biscuits! And most of the apples! And . . .".

"Come off it, Barry!" broke in Mike. The A.P.L. was exaggerating, yet Mike had eaten rather a lot that morning and was feeling a trifle guilty: the trouble was that the fresh air and all the trekking about gave him such an appetite.

The others laughed. They were in high spirits after showing a definite improvement in their map-reading and compass-work. With a little more practice they felt sure they would stand a good chance of winning the Troop Orienteering Competition, now three weeks away. There was a prize of two super new Continental tents for the winners and the Eagles' two ageing tents badly needed replacing.

They were in sight of Humblie's Wood and were following a bend in the road when four youths in black-leather jackets and riding Norton 500s roared down on them from behind.

"Look out, Eagles!" warned Alex, and they dived for safety into the hedgerow.

Joe Fox, the gang leader, screamed past Mike – who was always slower to move than any of the others – missing him by inches. Joe braked his machine savagely and skidded to a halt, sending clouds of dust and grit flying. His mates pulled sharply up beside him.

Before the dust had time to settle, Alex stormed angrily up to the youths.

"What an idiotic way to behave! You might have killed someone!"

Joe was a big powerfully-built youth with a swarthy complexion and a mane of black hair. He got off his bike and walked up to Alex aggressively, obviously spoiling for a fight.

"Oh, yeh! And what are yer gonna do about it, eh, Scoutboy?" growled the gang leader.

His mates crowded round their leader and jeered at Alex.

"Go on, Scouty, show Joe what yer made of!" urged Harry, a short fat youth with a sallow pockmarked face.

"He's scared!" cried Johnny.

"Are yer scared, Scoutboy?" queried Joe, a huge sneering grin on his cracked dusty lips.

"One punch, I reckon, Joe, would just about finish 'im!" said Albert, a tall gangling youth with a scarred nose.

Alex was no coward; he knew that and the Eagles knew that. Alex was also mature enough not to care what Joe and his mates thought of him. Alex had a responsibility to his Scouts and he had no intention of getting them involved in a totally unnecessary fight with – as far as he was concerned – a bunch of overgrown juvenile delinquents.

The Patrol Leader turned away. "Come on, Eagles, time we were getting back to camp. We've better things to do than waste time here."

The Scouts were angry, and would gladly have tackled the bigger and stronger youths without hesitation; however they recognised the value of discipline and doing what their leader told them. They had other ways of proving their courage than senseless fighting.

The Eagles marched off along the road, doing their best to ignore the taunts hurled after them.

"Scouts are cissies!"

"Cowards! Yah!"

"Run away before yer get hurt!"

Growing tired of jeering, the gang mounted their machines and hurtled off down the road. They had ropes with them and were heading for Black Hill, a huge column of cave-riddled rock in the wood not far from where the Scouts had pitched their camp. They were intending to climb the rock and explore the caves.

Unseen by the gang, several hundred yards away near the crossroads, Zeigler's Circus was approaching from a side road.

Joe raced ahead of his mates, urging every last rev from his 500 cc engine, revelling in the sheer excitement of speed. Each of the gang vied with the others in reckless daring acts, as they veered from side to side on the road trying to get ahead.

Trees lined the side of the road and hid the leading circus vehicle until it was too late. The van drove from the side road on to the main road, just as Joe reached the junction. Refusing to slacken speed, Joe heeled his bike over and sped in front of the van at 90 mph. Harry and Johnny followed suit fractions of a second later.

The van driver, seeing a collision with the last rider was inevitable, accelerated and swerved his van violently round as Albert flashed past. The van hit the fence at the side of the road and crashed through, dragging the trailer it was towing with it down the steep slope into the shallow pond there. The trailer hit a boulder and the impact burst the door open, releasing its frightened occupant.

Freddie, the performing Russian black bear, scampered away in terror; and before anyone could stop it the bear vanished into Humblie's Wood.

Unaware of what they had done the gang sped on, disappearing from view within seconds. A quarter of a mile further on they slowed and took the path that turned off into the wood.

Before long the Scouts arrived on the scene of the accident. They learned from one of the circus performers what had happened, but were assured that the bear was harmless unless provoked, in which case its great strength might prove dangerous.

Mario Zeigler, the circus owner, a big red-haired man, was in a flaming temper at the loss of his star performer, Freddie. Zeigler was rushing about trying to organise a party of men to hunt for the bear.

"We gotta find Freddie! My circus is finished withouta him! Hurry! Hurry! Getta ropes and nets!"

Zeigler was frantic and Alex had to speak to him three times before the circus owner noticed he was there.

"Can we help, Mr Zeigler? We know the wood well and we've done a bit of tracking in our time. We'll help you find Freddie, if you like."

Zeigler stared at Alex with an expression of astonishment and disbelief, as if he could scarcely believe his ears. Then he bellowed with laughter.

"You musta be joking! *You* help me finda *Freddie*, the great Russian bear who can benda iron bars and crush a man with one hug! Ho! Ho! Ho! Do not make me laugh! Run away home, little man, before you getta hurt! I finda Freddie myself!"

Zeigler turned away and rushed after his men, who were heading for the wood. "Waita for me!"

"Well, there's gratitude for you!" said Barry.

"He doesn't deserve to be helped with an attitude like that," said Mike, so annoyed he had forgotten about his empty stomach.

"Don't take it too hard, Eagles, he's obviously got a lot on his mind. No doubt it's a big responsibility running a circus, and when you lose your star turn it must be worrying. He doesn't realise what we're capable of either." Alex could be a real philosopher when he wanted to, and he had the knack of putting things in their proper perspective when they didn't run too well for the Scouts. He was a born leader and they respected him and his judgment.

"Yes, you're right, Alex. Silly of us to get worked up about it," agreed Barry.

"Gosh, I'm ravenous!" said Mike, remembering.

"Let's get back to camp and cook ourselves a slap-up feed. We can't have Mike starving, can we now, Eagles?"

Alex knew how to make them laugh. It was just as well, otherwise they might have been in quite a mood after being abused by the motor-cyclists and rebuffed by Zeigler.

They headed through the wood, not over concerned about Freddie being loose. They were reassured by the fact that the bear was harmless unless provoked, and since they were not in the habit of provoking bears it didn't worry them too much. Besides, the bear had apparently entered the southern part of the wood as that was the direction Zeigler and his men had taken. Their camp was well to the north and they felt sure the animal would soon be recaptured.

A shock awaited them at their camp, however.

It was wrecked. The tents were in ribbons. Their equipment strewn everywhere.

"Gosh!" groaned Mike, surveying with a woeful expression the remains of a week's supply of food.

"Crumbs!" said Peter, his mouth hanging open.

"What's happened?" said Barry.

"I'll tell you what has happened. Freddie's paid us a visit! Look there by the tents – claw marks." Alex pointed to where his keen eye had spotted their intruder's trademark.

"But Zeigler and his men went off to the south," said Barry.

"They've lost the bear's trail completely," mused Alex, thoughtfully eyeing the spoor marks leading off through the trees towards Black Hill.

This was their chance to show Zeigler what they were made of. They guessed what Alex was thinking, and he had barely begun to suggest, "I think we should find Freddie, Eagles," when they chorused their agreement.

"The way the bear is heading it will probably end up at Black Hill. If that happens it could well go to ground in one of the caves. Let's find out."

Alex quickly organised them for the hunt. They made sure they had their torches in their rucsacs and they salvaged their ropes from the disaster that was their camp.

The trail took a winding course through the wood, stopping at trees and stones: it was plain that Freddie had been in no hurry to get anywhere and was enjoying his new-found freedom.

A BC Cub? Seven-year-old Clayton Morris of Bath won first prize as Tutankhamen at the Bathwick School Fête and the Larkhall Scout Carnival.

STOP PRESS

The Eagles were only a short distance away from Black Hill when they heard an ominous sound: the deep-throated roar of powerful motor-cycle engines.

Minutes later the gang appeared, cavorting madly between the trees on their machines. Joe saw the Scouts and shouted to his mates. The four riders deliberately speeded up as they converged on the Patrol.

"Run 'em down!" yelled Joe, heading directly towards Alex.

The Scouts scrambled for cover for the second time that day as the gang hurtled past along the path the Scouts had been following. They were looking back and jeering when Alex spotted the bear crossing in front of Joe.

"Look out! In front of you!" yelled Alex.

Too late, Joe turned his head and saw Freddie. On the narrow path between the trees he had no room to manoeuvre at the speed he was travelling. Joe braked hard, his tyres refused to hold on the slippery leaf-strewn ground, and he slewed violently round, lost control and crashed into a tree. The three behind him did likewise. There was a tremendous crash and noise of buckling metal. The bear roared in fright and fled.

For a few moments the Scouts stood in stunned silence, watching the scene; then they rushed to help.

Luckily for the gang the worst that had happened was Johnny's broken leg. Harry had a sprained knee. Albert had a twisted shoulder. Joe had escaped virtually unscathed apart from a few bruises. It could have been a lot more serious. The four Nortons, collectively worth over a thousand pounds, were a tangled mass of twisted chrome, bent forks and broken exhaust pipes.

To the Eagles it was poetic justice. The gang had been more than amply rewarded for their misdeeds.

For a time Joe and his mates could only sit and glumly survey the wreckage, oblivious of their injuries. Then the shock wore off and the pain started.

To the gang's astonishment the Scouts offered to help, and they were too much in a daze to do anything but murmur grudging assent.

Alex and Barry soon had Johnny's leg in a rough splint. After all they had said and tried to do to the Scouts, this act shook their self-confidence to no little extent. This was unexpected behaviour to them, and they didn't quite know what to make of it yet.

"Well, that should hold you until you can see a doctor. It's a clean break and should mend quickly," said Alex, tying the last make-shift bandage into place.

The Patrol Leader explained how Freddie came to be in the wood. By this time resentment and anger were building up in the youths

at the damage to their machines. They had to find something or someone to blame and it wasn't going to be themselves. So they picked on the circus.

"Idiots should have stopped! We was on the main road, they was comin' out of the side road!" growled Joe.

"That's right, Joe! We had the right of way!" agreed Harry, ruefully rubbing his knee.

It was of little concern to the Scouts at that moment who had had the right of way; the bear had to be found, and quickly, before it did any more damage.

To their surprise Joe agreed to help. He was the only one of the gang in any fit state to and despite his misgivings about tackling the bear he couldn't appear a coward in the Scouts' eyes – especially after how he had taunted them. Joe was also motivated by a desire for revenge on the animal that had cost him so dear. His confidence was also bolstered when the Scouts informed him that the animal was harmless, as far as they knew.

Albert was sent off to find Zeigler and to get help for Johnny. Joe collected his rope and followed the Eagles as they picked up the bear's spoor again. The trail led off through the wood, over ground that left few marks, so that all the Eagles' skills in sign-reading had to be mustered.

They went south, then west, then south again, and finally north until they lost the spoor on the rocky base of Black Hill. An intensive search around the base of the rock showed no signs of the animal having gone off in another direction.

"Freddie is in one of the caves, I'll bet," said Mike, scanning the seventy-feet-high rock.

"The best course of action is to spread out round Black Hill and wait for Zeigler," said Alex.

"No, I think we should go in an' flush 'im out," argued Joe. "If the brute's as 'armless as yer say there's nothin' to be scared abat, is there?"

He was deliberately challenging them again. Alex argued that Joe was a fool, but the gang leader refused to listen. Joe had made up his mind and there was no changing it.

"I'm goin' in alone then," said Joe. "If yer scared stay 'ere and I'll send 'im out to yer."

Alex was beginning to be suspicious of the youth's real intentions towards the animal. The P.L. had no desire to see the animal harmed in any way, so he relented, against his better judgment.

"All right, Joe, I'll come in with you," said Alex.

The Eagles wanted to accompany their leader but Alex allowed only Barry to come, ordering the younger Scouts to remain on watch outside. Mike was sent to find Zeigler and direct him to Black Hill.

Alex and Barry removed their rucsacs to give them more freedom, then armed themselves with a rope and torch apiece. Joe took Bert's rope, and Peter loaned him a torch.

There was a fairly steep slope leading up to a ledge some twenty feet above the ground. There they discovered several small openings in the rock, though none large enough to enter by. Halfway round the rock they came upon a large cave. Some earth had collected by the entrance and there was a clear imprint of a bear's claw.

"This must be where Freddie's gone in," said Barry.

"Be careful, we don't want to do anything to alarm him," cautioned Alex.

Their hearts fluttered as they entered the cave and the darkness closed around them. The air was cold and damp, the atmosphere clammy and oppressive. They flashed their torches around but there was no sign of the bear.

The cave wound down into the heart of Black Hill, then branched into a number of tunnels. For the best part of an hour they searched the rabbit-warren, finding nothing to indicate where the animal had gone.

Joe's patience was soon exhausted; he lacked the Scouts' discipline and ability to persevere when things were not going right.

"I'm fed up with this," grumbled the gang leader eventually, utterly weary of their fruitless hunt. "The brute could be anywhere down 'ere. You can please yerselves, but I'm packin' it in."

There was no point in trying to make him

STOP PRESS

In 1967 the Commissioner in Wigan suggested to Mrs. Jean Pocock that perhaps she would look after a Cub Pack until somebody else could be found. She is still there. Nothing special about that, you may think, many of us are 'conned' in a similar way. But you would be wrong, for Mrs. Pocock is a paraplegic and has been confined to a wheelchair since 1952. Through her undaunted courage she runs an efficient Pack and leads them in many creative activities. For her services she has been awarded the Chief Scout's Certificate for Meritorious Conduct.

change his mind, as the Scouts had learned previously. He was going back to the surface and that was that.

Joe headed off on what he thought was the way they had come, though, unlike the Scouts, he had neglected to make careful note of what turns they had made and how many. He was soon hopelessly lost, and found himself descending deep into the heart of the rock.

Meanwhile Alex and Barry pursued their search. A good half-hour had passed since they parted from Joe when they came to a small passage with several openings. Alex stopped suddenly, listening.

"Barry, quiet a minute! Do you hear anything?"

"No – I don't think so . . . Wait a minute, you are right, Alex, it's coming from over there. That second opening to the left of us, I think."

The two Scouts entered the tunnel and soon came to a huge cavern. The walls sparkled green and cold in their torchlight.

Not far from where they stood was the bear, a rope around its neck, pacing angrily to and fro beneath a pillar of rock about ten feet high upon which shivered an exceedingly frightened Joe.

"H-help!" the youth stuttered through chattering teeth. "The brute's t-trying t-to eat me!"

Every few seconds Freddie rose on his hind legs and reached up to Joe, sniffing and growling at the cowering youth.

"Don't panic, Joe!" assured Alex. "We'll get you out of this. Only don't panic!"

It was fairly obvious how the youth had got himself into this predicament. Stumbling on Freddie, he had tried to capture the bear and show how brave and fearless he was, but his efforts had misfired, forcing him to take refuge from the enraged animal.

The Scouts' problem was what to do to save what could become a very messy situation. The bear was ignoring them for the moment, being too engrossed with Joe, and so giving them time to think. Whatever they did it had to be something that wouldn't antagonise the bear still more.

They racked their brains for a solution.

Then Alex had a brainwave.

"Barry, have you got your harmonica with you?"

"Yes, it's in my pocket, what do you want it for?"

"It's only a wild chance, I know, but anything is worth trying. Can you play the *Entry of the Gladiators*?"

"Of course!" replied Barry, tumbling to Alex's idea. "The tune they always play at the circus!"

Barry was pretty good on his harmonica and he soon produced a fair version of the tune.

To their astonishment the tune had a remarkable effect on the bear. Freddie had always done his act to the Gladiators' tune and had been so well trained that he automatically forgot Joe and went into his circus routine.

The bear paraded, bowed, turned somersaults, stood on its head, going through his complicated act for a good ten minutes as Barry played fast and furious encouraged by a jubilant Alex and a much relieved Joe.

They clapped and cheered as the bear stopped and bowed again. Cautiously Alex approached the animal as Barry continued to play. The Scout had a cake of chocolate and he offered it to Freddie. The bear took the cake and chewed greedily.

"Get down, Joe, slowly, and don't do anything stupid," ordered Alex. "I think Freddie has calmed down now."

"Friendly fellow, isn't he," said Barry, taking a well-earned breather.

With Barry harmonising on his harmonica, Alex took the rope Joe had so thoughtfully attached to Freddie's neck and led the bear out of the caves towards the surface. A greatly chastened Joe trailed at the rear. He admitted reluctantly to himself that he had underestimated the Scouts to a fatal extent. They had made him look a proper Charlie. Still he was very grateful to them for getting him out of a very awkward predicament.

Joe left Black Hill a sadder but wiser youth.

When the trio reached the outside it was to find Mike approaching, leading Zeigler and his men.

Freddie's trainer took charge of the animal and led him away to safe-keeping. Zeigler was immensely relieved and pleased to have his star performer returned to him unharmed.

"Magneeficent! You are all magneeficent!" he cried.

Mike had already told Zeigler what the bear had done to their camp and to the gang's motor-cycles. As a reward to the Scouts Zeigler handed Alex a cheque for fifty pounds to buy new equipment. The circus boss thought Joe and his mates had been punished enough – secretly he wasn't too keen on the idea of pressing charges of reckless driving as the motor-cyclists, in theory, had had the right of way on the main road. As a slight consolation Zeigler gave the gang free ringside tickets for the circus's next performance.

If there was one thing the gang had learned it was to be wary of circuses and Scouts in future.

"You must all a come to the next show and see the great Freddie performing his fantastic act," enthused Zeigler, as they all headed off through the wood. "You have never seen such a performance as my Freddie gives! It is magneeficent!"

Alex laughed inwardly. He already had and it had been free, too!

The Chief Scout

Sir William Gladstone Bt, DL, MA,

On Wednesday, July 26th 1972, in St. James' Palace in London, the Council of The Scout Association met. The purpose of the meeting was to elect the new Chief Scout of the United Kingdom Overseas Branches to succeed Lord Maclean. Many long hours had been spent before the meeting trying to find one man who had all the qualities that the position of Chief Scout demanded. Finally that man was found—Sir William Gladstone, the great grandson of William Gladstone the Prime Minister. In the next few pages you can find out a little more about our Chief Scout.

Sir William is a keen family man. The Chief and Lady Gladstone watch their children at play in the gardens.

One of the family 'pets' is this donkey, ridden by Vicky. Robert is leading the donkey. Charles is already a Cub Scout with his local Pack.

Two other family pets are Sir William's labradors.

Charles is naturally proud of his father's new position, and enjoys telling him about his test work progress!

Besides reading history and working on his estate, the Chief has a great interest and skill in woodwork.

Fond of children and animals, the Chief is teaching his daughter Vicky to ride from an early age!

A photograph is as good a reason as any to pause in the tiring business of scything long grass.

A careful and skilled gardener, the Chief neglects no part of his estate. Even trees need regular attention.

The Chief has a large greenhouse in which he grows all sorts of flowers.

The Chief is also very fond of animals. He takes good care of all wild life—here he is seen with one of the ducks from his estate.

The Chief spends a lot of time working on his estates. He gave up teaching so that he could give more attention to his farmlands.

As you have seen from this feature, the Chief is very interested in the things that you are interested in, and in the things that you do. One day you may well meet him—he plans to travel about a lot in his new position as Chief Scout. Of course, it is not really correct to refer to him as our 'new' Chief Scout—he has held the position for over a year now. A task of such importance, however, takes a lot of getting used to, and the Chief is counting on every one of us to support him throughout the time he leads us. We wish him many happy and successful years as 'Our Chief'.

Photographed by Jack Olden
and Harold Wyld

Adventure into STEAM

Our chartered train, 75027, at Sheffield Park Station, just before its journey to Horsted Keynes complete with 190 Cub Scouts.

Written and photographed by Lawrence Curtis

190 Cub Scouts from Newham East in London, filled four coaches and made their way through busy London into the peaceful Sussex countryside to the headquarters of the famous preservation railway, the Bluebell Line, at Sheffield Park Station, near Uckfield, Sussex.

For this was the start of an adventure into the world of steam, as the Bluebell Railway, using standard railway gauge, runs a passenger carrying service from Sheffield Park Station to Horsted Keynes Station, some six miles away, with Freshfield Halt as a 'request stop'.

They only use steam engines, obtained from British Rail. One engine, Fenchurch, is 100 years old and at the time of our visit it was being overhauled and re-painted. The Bluebell is the only engine painted in its own livery and in constant use for daily services.

At Sheffield Park arrangements were made for the

Cub Scouts to visit the museum (a converted waiting room), the signal box and the engine sheds. They also had the opportunity to go on to the footplate of one of the stationary engines in the sheds.

The grand moment arrived when the specially chartered train arrived to transport us to Horsted Keynes. (Due to the size of our party we could not use the coaches laid on for public service.) Thanks to an anonymous donor the 75027 engine was saved from the cutter's torch when steam ended on British Rail in 1968, and this ensured that an example of the ultimate in modern design was preserved for posterity on the Bluebell Railway.

Horsted Keynes was full of adventure: we were able to inspect our engine, sit on the driver's seat and pull the whistle cord! We also asked the footplatemen lots of questions. The coach sheds were explored and we met many of the voluntary workers repairing the old and damaged coaches recently acquired for future use. All but six of the Bluebell staff are unpaid and devote a great deal of their spare time to the preservation of the line.

As you can see from the photographs there are plenty of places to see and explore. Your Cub Leader will be able to arrange a visit which will give you an experience never to be forgotten – a look at the world of steam!

Signalman Dave Phillips in control at Sheffield Park box.

Engine driver Tommy Dobson – whose full-time job is a pilot with BOAC on VC10's – shows one of the many Cubs the driver's eye view.

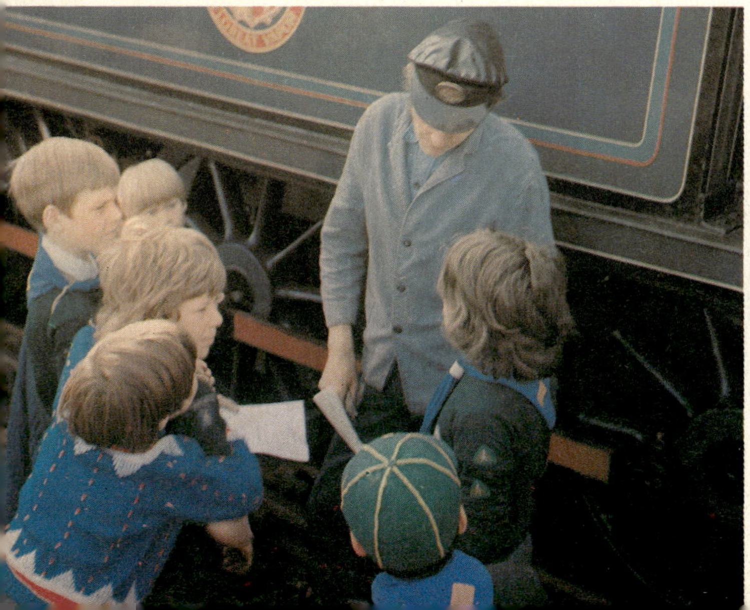

Fenchurch, the 100-year-old engine, meets with the approval of the Cubs in its new paintwork.

Some of the Cubs with one of the footplatemen by the famous Bluebell Engine, the only engine painted in its own livery.

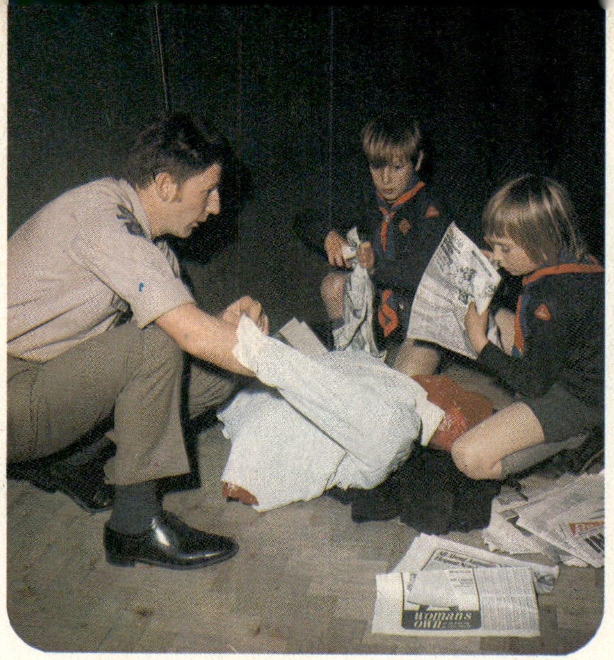

Under the instruction of their Cub Scout Leader, these Cubs 'stuff' the guy's body with plenty of newspaper.

The Cubs design and draw their own face for the guy.

REMEMBER THE GUY?

photographed by Lawrence Curtis

For many weeks before 5th November, Cub Scouts like these, members of 65th Hackney (St. George's) Cub Pack, make preparations for an evening of making guys.

All the Cub Packs in the Hackney District join together for a combined Guy Fawkes celebration which is held at Gilwell Park. All the guys are placed upon a giant bonfire and fireworks, supplied by the Cub Scouts, are ignited by the Cub Scout Leaders. Supervision such as this prevents accidents and it also makes for a better display.

In the remnants of one of your jumble sales you should be able to find suitable clothes for a guy which, stuffed with plenty of paper, will look almost human and give a 'glowing' result!

If you are planning a firework party, Akela will be able to tell you about the Firework Code which is published every year by the Firework Makers Guild.

A discarded wig is found which is used for the guy's hair.

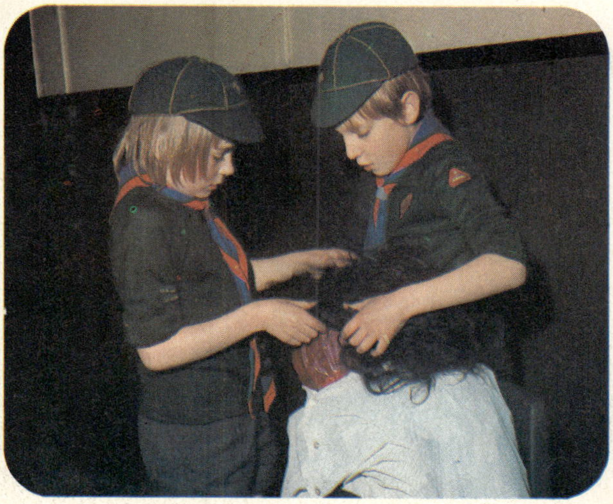

Me and my guy, and a safety firework, the sparkler.

EUROPEAN Pack Meetings

by David P. Saint
Photos by Bill Carden and Ed Lucas

1972 was European Friendship Year and many Scout Troops organised exchange visits or international camps with Scouts from abroad. Many Venture Scouts also visited other countries to find out more about their ways of life. Much thought was given to the way Cub Scouts could share in the activities, and in SCOUTING, the National Magazine of the Scout Association, several ideas were put forward for Cub Scout European Evenings, and a number of Packs used these.

The 2nd Gerrards Cross (Thorpe House) and the 1st Holtspur (Spearhead) Packs combined for a Swiss Evening. All the Cubs had made passports, which were stamped when they arrived for the meeting. They then had to find Cantons (areas of Switzerland) on a large map of the country and mark them with the correct shield. A cut-up map of Switzerland was given to each Six and they had to put these together like a jigsaw – not so easy when you do not know the country and its shape!

These boys must be in the Swiss Passport Office having their papers checked! Above their heads you can see the map and the shields. After tea the evening finished with games, a quiz and a sing song, and it was obvious that the Cubs had thoroughly enjoyed their visit to Switzerland.

There was a big display about Switzerland for the Cubs to look at. I wonder how many items *you* can spot that are obviously from Switzerland?

If you know anything about foreign flags you will see that the 1st and 2nd Gerrards Cross Packs had a Dutch evening. They, too, had their passports stamped at the Customs Post on arrival and then stood at the Alert as the Dutch and English flags were broken.
There were lots of games to play, including one to fill a broken dyke, and a treasure hunt when the Cubs had to find lots of objects the first letters of which made up the key word AMSTERDAM.
After tea, when the Cubs sampled Edam Cheese, a lady from Holland gave an illustrated talk about her

country and brought a greeting from Dutch Cub Scouts written in Dutch. A talk about dairy produce and dairy farming by the Dairy Board followed, and the Cubs were given leaflets, flags and tulips as souvenirs.
Everyone obviously enjoyed the evening and learned a lot about another country.

The Cubs of the 162nd Liberton Pack in Edinburgh joined with some of the Troop to have a European Weekend. They were split into 'Nations', named after their national dish, while the Leaders formed a body which they called 'The Six'. Do you know why they called themselves that?
Unfortunately the weather prevented the Cubs spending much time out-of-doors, but when they were able to go out they took part in activities and games based on the Arrow tests. When indoors they worked on a European display project, which is to be finished later in the year, consisting of a large map showing the twenty-two European countries who have Scouts, each marked with a national flag, Scout Badge and other relevant symbols.
On the Saturday evening there was a camp fire with an international flavour – some songs were even sung in foreign languages.
The final event of the weekend was the European Games, prior to which there was a parade of teams with national flags.
It was quite a different sort of camp for the boys, and one which was greatly enjoyed.

THE MUDLARK

by Sylvia E. Baxendale

Robert came home from camp today,
He went in the bathtub right away.
There was mud in his hair and round his toes,
Behind his ears and all over his nose.
And you should see his clothes!

"Have you washed yourself while you've been away?"
"I went in the river on Wednesday,
And I washed some clothes in the river as well."
"That would account for their colour and smell.
"I thought you could tell."

"There's mud in my 'jamas, and mud in my bed,
And I'm covered with gnat bites right up to my head.
My blankets got wet through a hole in the tent,
I cut both my knees, and my penknife's all bent,
My torch has a dent.
But I'm glad that I went."

It'll take him a week to get himself clean,
So Mummy says, if you know what I mean,
But he's looking so well and feeling so fit,
She doesn't mind Robert and all his kit.
So that's it.

GOOD TEAMWORK

"Go home, Blacks!" said the poster the young lads were carrying.

It was a gloomy afternoon in North London and Shirley and Lorna were on their way to Guides.

"I wish they wouldn't carry these things around and write them on walls," said Lorna. "There's a very nice girl in my class and she's black. She must feel terrible when she sees words like that."

"I think it's all wrong," said Shirley. "The other day Mum tripped as she was going on to a bus and the black conductor was so good to her. But when the bus was full and he couldn't allow any more people on, they were all shouting at him: 'Go home, black!' It's so stupid and so cruel. I wish we could do something about it. But it's like everything else. We carry first-aid kits and money for the phone and we try to be the friends of all, but we never seem to get a chance to do anything."

"Well, I suppose we could challenge these boys," said Lorna, "but I feel scared."

"Actually, I know one of them," said Shirley, looking at them as they passed on the other side of the street. It's John Redmond. He used to be in Scouts with my brother, David, but he left long ago. He was annoyed when some black boys joined the Troop. I remember David was furious with him. I wouldn't like to tackle him, I'm afraid. He's got into rather bad company now."

"Look out, Shirley," said Lorna suddenly, pulling her friend by the arm. A huge car had just come round the corner behind them and was tearing along the street.

"He's mad, going at that speed," said Lorna. There'll be an accident before long. Anyway, I've got his number, if anything happens." Her quick eyes had noted it and she had managed to get it down in her notebook.

"Oh, look!" said Shirley. "Someone's been

knocked down, just along by the dress shop. Come on, we must run and see what we can do."

The two girls dashed along the street. Just outside the shop on the pavement a man was lying. The car must have mounted the pavement at that point. His arm was bleeding badly and his leg looked as if it had been damaged.

"We mustn't move him," said Shirley. "He might have broken something. We'll have to get an ambulance and a policeman. One of us had better go and do that."

"But we must stop the bleeding first," said Lorna," and it's very bad. I think we should both do that. Surely some passerby will ring for an ambulance."

The street was very quiet but there was a well-dressed gentleman walking along towards them.

"Oh, sir," said Lorna, "would you help us, please. We want an ambulance to take this poor man to hospital and we can't leave him because he's bleeding badly. Could you ring for one, please."

"I'm very sorry," said the gentleman, raising his hat, "but, you know, Board meetings won't wait. I'm already late. Sorry not to help." He had gone.

"There's a lady standing by the dress shop window," said Shirley, "let's ask her."

"I'm afraid I can't manage," was the reply. "I really must get into the shop before it closes. I do so want that dress. It might be gone if I left it till tomorrow. So sorry!" She flashed a smile and turned away.

The two girls were standing by the man, taking turns in pressing on his arm to try to stop the bleeding. What were they to do? The street ahead was deserted. Just then they heard a boy's voice coming from behind them. they looked. There were the boys with the placard.

Scouts 'have courage in all difficulties', and so do Cub Scouts. Ten year old Craig Brownlie, a Cub Scout in Frimley, was sixth out of sixty-nine in an official Cycling Proficiency Test organised by the Accident Prevention Society and the Police. He plays football for his Pack and is learning to swim. So what, you may say: Craig was born a thalidomide baby and has only one leg.

"Are you in trouble?" It was John Redmond speaking. "Can I do something?"

"Oh yes, please, John," said Shirley. "This poor man was knocked down by that madman in the car. You must have seen him, and he's bleeding very badly. Lorna and I have to take turns in pressing on his arm and holding his head off the pavement. We can't leave him and we need an ambulance and a policeman."

"He's a black," called one of the gang. "Don't bother with him, John. Come on! If a copper comes, we're for it!"

"Sorry, girls," said another more gently, "but you're wasting your time with a chap like that."

"Just a minute!" said John, looking down at the poor man. "He's a human being after all and he needs help. I'll go and dial 999."

"You can count me out," said one of the gang, slinking away.

"Me, too," said another.

But four stayed.

"Dick, you go and fetch that copper we were avoiding," said John. "He went down towards the Post Office. I'll dial for the ambulance."

Dick went off. One of the others, Jim, took off his anorak and folded it under the man's head. Bill tied a bandage, according to Shirley's instructions, round the man's arm. Lorna's face was anxious as she pressed on the nearest pressure point to the wound but the bleeding was definitely easing off.

John had returned. "I'll come to the hospital with you," he said unexpectedly. "That car driver was mad. We all thought something was sure to happen. Wish I'd taken his number!"

"We've got it," said Shirley. "Lorna took it. She's written it down.

"Good for you!" said John. "I always thought Guides learnt something. Maybe I'd have done better to stay in Scouts. Poor chap! Look, he's trying to speak. What is it, sir?" John bent down to the man.

"Thank you, my friends," the man was whispering. "What happened?"

"You were knocked down," said Lorna, "but don't worry! We'll come to hospital with you. The ambulance is on the way."

"My wife!" said the man faintly.

"We'll go to see her and explain," said Bill. "Where does she live?"

"2, Gaylord's Buildings," whispered the man. "Her name's Freeman. I can't thank you enough."

"Never mind about that," said Bill and they were off.

"What's going on here?" said a deep voice.

It was the policeman, accompanied by Dick. "Poor chap! Sent for an ambulance? Good! Got the number of the car? Great crowd you are!"

"Oh, that was the Guides!" said John. "They were clever enough to get that."

"And what might this be?" asked the policeman, seeing the placard.

"Oh, please forget about it," begged John. "It was ours, but I think we'll be getting rid of it."

The wail of the ambulance siren could be heard now and there it was. The men got out and expertly carried the poor man into the ambulance. John and the two girls got in, too. Dick agreed to go to the Guide Hall and explain to Captain where the girls were.

Soon the man was tucked up in bed in hospital and his wife had arrived, escorted by Bill. Jim had stayed in the flat with the two little girls.

"Come with me, Mrs. Freeman," said a nurse very kindly. "Your husband is going to be all right. These girls did very well. They coped marvellously with the bleeding arm. Just a week or so in bed and he'll be as right as rain."

"You've been so good to my husband," said Mrs. Freeman, her face smiling now. "And your friend is with my little girls. I do hope they'll be all right."

"Don't worry," said Shirley. "We'll go and play with them till you come home from hospital. Do stay with your husband as long as you can."

The Freeman's flat was up a dark, smelly staircase. Nothing seemed to have been done to the property for a long time. The flat itself was in a bad state of decoration and repair. Jim was standing by the window, trying to comfort little Eliza and Louise. Eliza, the elder of the two, had her arm round the little sister. They were both crying.

"Don't cry!" said Shirley. "We've all come to play with you, and Mummy will soon be home. Tomorrow you'll see Daddy. He's feeling fine."

Soon they were all the best of friends. What a wonderful romp it was for Eliza and Louise, and then Mrs. Freeman was back.

"He's feeling much better," she said. "I'm so relieved. You've been so kind to us. My husband wanted me to thank you properly."

"We'll go to the hospital to see him," said Shirley. "I'm so glad he's feeling comfortable. They'll be very good to him in hospital."

John had been looking round the dark, miserable room.

"Mrs. Freeman," he said, "how do you feel about us giving your husband a surprise when he comes home? I'd like to try and decorate your flat for you, if you'd let me, and I'm sure my pals would help."

"Good idea, John," said Dick. "We'd enjoy that."

"My Dad's a decorator," said John, "and I've often helped him. We could get the paint and paper from our shop, too."

Mrs. Freeman's eyes filled with tears. "That would be marvellous," she said. "But we couldn't afford it at the moment."

"But you don't have to," said John. "That will be our pleasure. It's the Easter holidays and we've tons of time. We'll be along tomorrow evening with the stuff."

"And we'll be here, too," said Shirley. "We'll make some new curtains and cushions to match the new decorations. To think of the times we've looked for a job like this to do!"

What a hive of activity the Freeman's flat was most evenings that week! John and Dick were up on ladders and planks painting the walls and ceiling. Jim and Bill were the painters of doors and skirting boards, and in another room Mrs. Freeman, helped by Shirley and Lorna and two of their friends from Guides, sewed curtains and gay new cushion covers. Little Eliza and Louise had their jobs too, holding pins for turning up hems and fetching and carrying for all the helpers.

It was such fun when they paused for a teabreak. Mrs. Freeman told them such interesting tales of Ghana, where they had come from, and she was full of jokes now that she knew her husband was getting on so well and would soon be home.

In hospital Peter Freeman had no idea of what was going on in his flat. He knew the young people were keeping an eye on his family, but that was all. One day little Eliza nearly let the cat out of the bag.

"Our flat's lovely now, Daddy," she said.

Quickly nudging her, her mother said: "Yes, it is. What a difference young folk like our friends make to it. They're so good to Eliza and Louise. Eliza is going to Brownies next week. Lorna and Shirley have bought her a uniform and Louise is longing for the day when she'll be old enough to go, too."

At last the great day came. Peter was coming home. He was speechless when he entered the flat.

"Do you like it, dear?" said his wife. "This is a present from our young friends. They've been so good and tomorrow night we're having a party for them."

What a party it was! "I can't thank you friends enough," said Peter.

"You needn't try," said John. "We've had a great time. I've never enjoyed myself so much in my life!"

"Neither have we!" said Shirley. "And it's so interesting now to have friends from Ghana."

"John's back at Scouts," said David the next week, as he and Shirley sat at supper with their parents. "He's brought three other chaps with him, too. I can't think why he came, but he's as keen as mustard. He's even talking of bringing a black chap along. I thought he was against black people."

"Not now," said Shirley, smiling. "I can tell you all about that."

Keeping in top physical shape is an important part of astronaut training. Each astronaut selects his own way of maintaining shape. A gym at the Manned Spacecraft Centre is always open for them. *Working out are, left to right, former Second Class Scout Eugene A. Cernan, former Scout Edwin E. Aldrin, Jr., and former Cub and Star Scout Thomas P. Stafford.*

THE SCOUT ASTRONAUTS

Mitchell R. Sharpe, a former Cub and Boy Scout, is an American science writer who specialises in space subjects. He has had two books, Living in Space and Satellites and Probes, published by Aldus Books Ltd. Among his friends are several of the former Scouts and Astronauts about whom he writes in this article.

"That's one small step for man, one giant leap for mankind," said former Eagle Scout Neil A. Armstrong as he stepped onto the surface of the Moon, the first man to do so, on 20th July 1969. Only nineteen minutes later he was joined by the second man to walk on the Moon, former Scout Edwin E. Aldrin, Jr. Two more pioneers followed them to the Moon only four months later. They were also former Scouts: Cub Scout Charles (Pete) Conrad and First Class Scout Alan L. Bean.

In all seventy-two men have been named to the American civil astronaut programme, and fifty-five of them were Scouts. Among the sixty-four active and former astronauts are forty-seven Scouts. Since the beginning of the manned space-flight programme, eight astronauts have been killed in accidents or operational training; all of them, too, were Scouts.

THE REASON WHY

There are many reasons why you find so many Scouts among the astronauts. Perhaps the most obvious one is that Scouts seek out adventure, and space exploration is the ultimate in adventure today. Also, Scouts are possessed with initiative, courage, and self-reliance. These are qualities which every astronaut must have. Finally, some of the things the Scout learns early and masters, are an integral part of the astronaut's training programme.

Take, for example, survival training. Astronauts must be able to sustain themselves until help arrives in any location on Earth if their spacecraft makes an emergency landing where there are no recovery forces. They all go through survival training, and it is a familiar routine for the former Scouts among them. It means living off the land in jungle and desert, and staying afloat in water.

Part of this training is done in the jungles of Panama, where the astronaut quickly learns which vines store drinkable water and which plants are edible. He also learns to skin a snake and eat it raw or cooked, if he can start a fire with flint and steel.

In the deserts of the American west, the astronaut learns to make Bedouin robes and tents of his parachute to protect him from the sun, and he learns to conserve his scanty emergency supply of water and food, too. Throughout this phase of training the astronaut must exhibit the ability to improvise in order to survive, another reason why Scouts make good astronauts.

MEET THE SCOUT ASTRONAUTS

Now let's take a look at some of the astronauts who were Scouts and see what they have done and what they will be doing in space as the world enters its second decade of manned space exploration.

Edwin E. Aldrin, Jr. was an active Scout in his home town of Montclair, New Jersey. His experience as an astronaut includes being pilot of the 4-day Gemini 12 mission in 1966 and also being the pilot of the Eagle spacecraft, first to land on the Moon on 20th July 1969.

William A. Anders, a Life Scout in La Mesa, California, was born in Hong Kong. He served as back-up (alternate) pilot on the Gemini 11 flight in 1966 and made his first and only spaceflight in man's first voyage around the Moon in Apollo 8 in December 1968. He is currently Secretary of the National Space Council, having resigned as an astronaut to accept this position.

Neil A. Armstrong, first man on the Moon and an Eagle Scout who finished his requirements for the rank after entering college, was a pilot of the X-15 rocket plane before becoming an astronaut in 1962. He was pilot of the Gemini 8 mission in 1966, which had a narrow brush with disaster when it went out of control, and he was commander of the Apollo 11 mission which landed on the Moon on 20th July 1969. Today, he is director of Aeronautical Research at the National Aeronautics and Space Administration. An Explorer Scout advisor, he has received the Order of the Arrow and the Order of the Buffalo.

Alan L. Bean, a First Class Scout from Texas, was the fourth man to set foot on the Moon as lunar module pilot of the Apollo 12. He was also back-up pilot on Gemini 10 in 1966 and back-up lunar module pilot on the Apollo 8 mission of 1968. He then began training for future missions in Earth-orbiting space stations.

Not all astronaut training is hard work. Following astronaut and former Life Scout Thomas K. Mattingly into the pool for scuba diving are astronaut and former Star Scout Richard F. Gordon, Jr., former Eagle Scout James A. Lovell, Jr., and former Second Class Scout John W. Young.

Scout training comes in handy for former Scouts among the astronauts when they take their desert survival training course. They learn to tear up their parachutes to make shelters and conserve their water supply until they can be rescued.

Neil A. Armstrong, first man on the Moon and former Eagle Scout, flew the X-15 rocket plane long before he became an astronaut.

Frank Borman, a Scout from Tucson, Arizona, became an astronaut in 1962 and served as back-up pilot on the Gemini 4 mission of 1965. Because of his extensive engineering background, he served on the board of experts that investigated the tragedy that took the lives of three of his fellow astronauts (and former Scouts) in January 1967. He served as pilot of the Gemini 7 mission, which orbited Earth for fourteen days in 1965, and commander of the Apollo 8 mission in 1968. He retired as an astronaut in 1970.

M. Scott Carpenter, a Cub and Boy Scout from Colorado, was one of the original seven astronauts accepted in 1959. He was pilot of the Mercury 7 mission in 1962, and in 1967 he returned to duty with the U.S. Navy to do underwater research, becoming in effect an aquanaut. He later retired from the Navy.

Eugene A. Cernan, Second Class Scout from Chicago, Illinois, was selected an astronaut in 1963. He was pilot on the Gemini 9 mission in 1966; back-up pilot for Gemini 12 flight in 1966; back-up pilot for the Apollo 7 mission in 1968; command module pilot of Apollo 10, which looped the Moon in 1969, after which he resumed training for future missions, including back-up commander of the Apollo 14 mission in 1971. He was pilot of the lunar module in the 1972 Apollo mission.

Charles (Pete) Conrad, Jr., the Cub Scout we met earlier, joined the astronaut corps in 1962. In 1965 he was pilot of the 8-day Gemini 5 flight; and in the following year he was command pilot of the 3-day Gemini 11 mission. As commander of the Apollo 12 mission in 1969, he became the third man to walk on the Moon, following which he began training for future missions in Earth-orbiting space stations.

Leroy G. Cooper, a Life Scout of Shawnee, Oklahoma, was one of America's original seven astronauts selected in 1959. He was the pilot of the Mercury 9 flight, final in that programme, and command pilot of the Gemini 5 mission, which spent seven days in space in 1965. He retired as an astronaut in 1970 after serving as back-up commander of the Apollo 10 mission in 1969.

Donn F. Eisele, an Eagle Scout and Air Scout as well, of Columbus, Ohio, became an astronaut in 1963 and served as command module pilot on the Apollo 7 mission of 1968. In 1970 he resigned as an astronaut to become a technical consultant in manned spaceflight at the Langley Research Centre of the National Aeronautics and Space Administration, in Virginia.

Joe H. Engle, a First Class Scout of Abilene, Kansas, was, like fellow Scout Armstrong, an X-15 rocket plane pilot before becoming an astronaut in 1966. He was a member of the astronaut support team for Apollo 10 in 1969 and back-up lunar module pilot for the Apollo 14 mission in 1971.

Ronald E. Evans, a Life Scout of St. Francis, Kansas, became an astronaut in 1966. A member of the support crew for the Apollo 7 mission in 1968 and the Apollo 11 mission in 1969, he was also the back-up command module pilot on Apollo 14 in 1971 and a member of the 1972 Apollo mission.

Richard F. Gordon, Jr., a Star Scout from Seattle, Washington, became an astronaut in 1963 and served as back-up pilot for the Gemini 8 flight in 1966, pilot of the 3-day Gemini 11 mission in 1966, back-up command module pilot of the Apollo 9 flight in 1969, and the command module pilot for the Apollo 12 mission in 1969. He was also back-up commander for the Apollo 15 mission in 1971.

Fred W. Haise, Jr., a Star Scout of Biloxi, Mississippi, was selected as an astronaut in 1966. He served as lunar module back-up pilot for the Apollo 8 mission in 1968 and the Apollo 11 flight in 1969. He was lunar module pilot of the ill-fated Apollo 13 mission of 1970 that nearly ended in disaster. On return to Earth he resumed training for future missions. He received the Scout's Pine Burr Award in his home town in 1970.

James A. Lovell, Jr., an Eagle Scout of Cleveland, Ohio, became an astronaut in 1962 and spent a total of thirty-eight days in space, more than any other American or Russian astronaut up to 1971. Lovell was pilot of the 14-day mission of Gemini 7 in 1965, command pilot of the 3-day Gemini 12 mission in 1966, lunar module pilot of the 3-day Apollo 8 mission in 1968, and commander of the 6-day Apollo 13 mission that ended in near tragedy in 1970. Lovell resigned as an astronaut in 1970.

James A. McDivitt, a Cub Scout and Boy Scout from Berlin, Wisconsin, became an astronaut in 1962. His first space mission was commander of the 4-day Gemini 4 mission in 1965. He was also commander of the 10-day Apollo 9 mission in 1969, following which he was appointed Apollo Programme Manager at the Manned Spacecraft Centre in Houston, Texas.

Edgar D. Mitchell, a Life Scout of Hereford, Texas, became a pilot astronaut in 1966 and holds a Ph.D. degree in aeronautics and astronautics. A member of the astronaut support team for the Apollo 9 mission in 1969, he was back-up lunar module pilot for the Apollo 10 mission in 1969. He was named lunar module pilot for the Apollo 14 mission in 1971.

Walter M. Schirra, Jr., a First Class Scout of Oradell, New Jersey, was one of the original seven astronauts selected in 1959. His flights included the 9-hour Mercury 8 mission of 1962, commander of the 1-day Gemini 6 mission in 1965, and commander of the 11-day Apollo 7 mission in 1968. He retired from the programme in 1969 to enter the business world.

Harrison H. Schmitt, a Scout of Silver City, New Mexico, was selected as a scientist-astronaut in 1965. He has a Ph.D. in geology and has received extensive training for manned lunar exploration missions. He was also back-up lunar module pilot for the Apollo 15 mission in 1971.

Russell L. Schweickart, a First Class Scout of Neptune, New Jersey, joined the astronauts in 1963 and served as lunar module pilot on the Apollo 9 flight in 1969, following which he began training for Earth-orbital missions.

David R. Scott, a Life Scout from San Antonio, Texas, became an astronaut in 1963 and was pilot of the 10-hour Gemini 8 mission in 1966 and command module pilot of the 10-day Apollo 9 mission in 1969. He was later named commander of the Apollo 15 mission in 1971.

Alan B. Shepard, Jr., a First Class Scout of East Derry, New Hampshire, is one of the original seven astronauts selected in 1959. After his sub-orbital flight in Freedom 7 in 1961, he was grounded for nine years because of a physical defect. Later this was corrected by surgery and he regained flight status and was named commander of the Apollo 14 mission in 1971.

Thomas P. Stafford, a Cub and Star Scout of Weatherford, Oklahoma, was selected as an astronaut in 1962. He was the pilot of the 1-day Gemini 6 mission, command pilot of the 3-day Gemini 9 flight in 1966, and commander of the 8-day Apollo 10 mission in 1969. He then became chief of the astronaut office at the Manned Spacecraft Centre in Houston, Texas, while keeping up his training for future missions.

John L. Sweigert, Jr., a Second Class Scout of Denver, Colorado, became an astronaut in 1966 and served as a member of the support crew for Apollo 7 in 1968 and the Apollo 11 flight in 1969. He was the command module pilot on the near-fatal Apollo 13 mission in 1970.

Alfred M. Worden, a First Class Scout of Jackson, Michigan, became an astronaut in 1966 and served on the support crew for the Apollo 9 mission in 1969. He was back-up command module pilot for the Apollo 12 mission in 1969. He was also command module pilot for the Apollo 15 mission in 1971.

John W. Young, a Second Class Scout from Orlando, Florida, joined the astronauts in 1962. He served as pilot on the first orbital mission in the Gemini series in 1965 and was command pilot for the 3-day Gemini 10 mission in 1966. He was the back-up command module pilot for the Apollo 7 mission in 1968 and command module pilot on the 8-day Apollo 10 flight in 1969.

These, then, are the astronauts today. As man begins to probe beyond long-term, Earth-orbiting space stations and permanent settlements on the Moon as well as expeditions to Mars, we will see succeeding generations of astronauts, and undoubtedly the majority of them will also be Scouts.

Edwin E. Aldrin, Jr., left, former Scout and second man to walk on the Moon, goes through training with fellow astronaut and former Eagle Scout Neil A. Armstrong, first man on the Moon. They practise picking up rocks as they later would on the lunar surface.

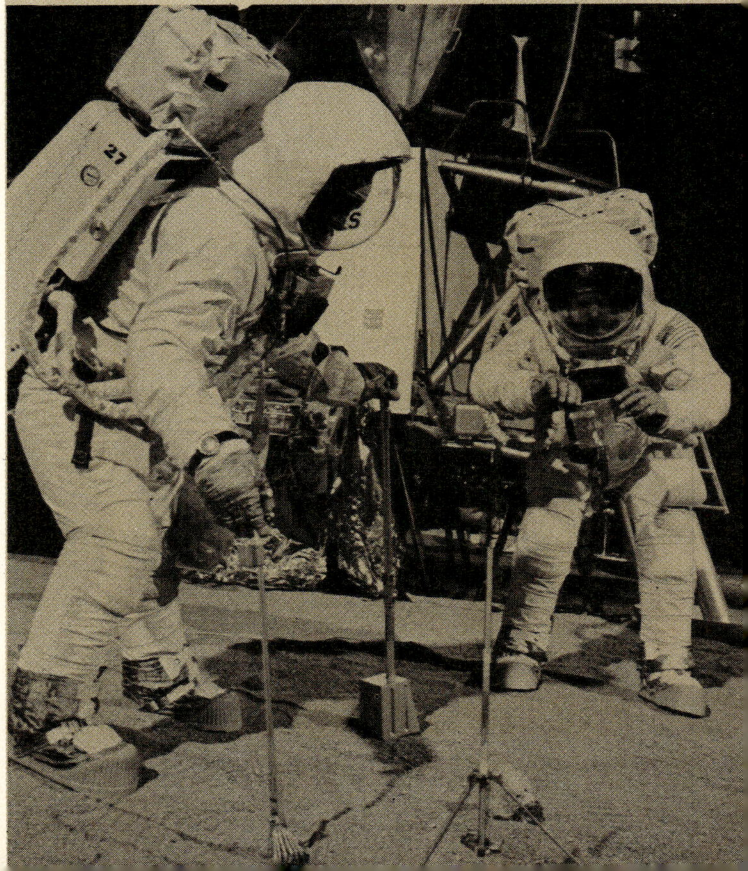

THE RESCUE OF MICHAEL

"You're in charge now, Peter," said Akela. "Off you go whenever you're ready."

Peter, Sixer of the Black Six of the 1st Frampton Pack, looked round. The small dinghy in which he was sitting with Bill, his Second, and Akela, seemed in order. He glanced aloft. The jibsail, tended by Bill, and the mainsail, the sheet of which he held, seemed to be set correctly. He looked up and down the river. There were no boats moving which he could foul.

"All right," said the Sixer, "push off, Bill."

The Second did as he was told and the wind caught the sails of the dinghy.

Peter felt the mainsheet and tiller in his hand come alive and the dinghy surged downriver. The wind direction called for a tack and Peter sent the dinghy towards the opposite river bank. There were a few craft tied up by the riverside hotel, but downriver lay the emptiness of river, marsh and woods.

Peter maintained the tack until the last moment and then, with an order to Bill, thrust the tiller away from himself. The bow of the dinghy swung round to take up a fresh tack, but at that moment an extra puff of wind seemed to check the way of the boat. The bow of the dinghy bumped the side of a moored motor cruiser.

The dinghy had only moved away a few yards when a man and a woman, aroused by the sound of the impact, appeared on deck.

The man looked over the side, could see no damage, but shouted furiously: "What are you

kids playing at! Keep away! D'you hear? And you," the man continued, pointing at Akela, "you ought to know better than to let them smash our boat!"

"Sorry," shouted Akela, "it was only a tap. I don't think you'll find any damage."

The man scowled and said no more. The dinghy sailed on downstream. "Sorry, Akela," muttered Peter, "my fault all right."

"Oh, don't worry," said Akela, "it could happen to the best of us. Now just concentrate on tacking downstream."

Peter did so, after taking a last guilty look over his shoulder at the motor cruiser, with its name 'Amanda' inscribed prominently on its bow. The river connecting Wareham to Poole Harbour wound tortuously to and fro. There appeared to be no life on the deserted sedges bordering the river.

Akela, Peter and Bill were planning to spend the weekend exploring some of the remote creeks and islands of the area. Akela had obtained permission to camp for the night on one of the islands and the dinghy's limited stowage was carefully packed with lightweight camping gear. Their progress was slow, the winding river demanding many tacks. At last, however, the river broadened into the great expanse of Poole Harbour. The setting sun sent shimmering light across the ruffled surface. Free from the shelter of woodlands bordering the river the wind felt strong and Peter enjoyed the sensation of a long and fast reach.

"That's the island," called Akela, pointing forward. "Steer to starboard a little. That's it! We'll soon be ashore now."

It was not long before the dinghy bumped a patch of shingle.

Bill called out: "Not bad, skipper! Your navigation is marvellous. You hit the island first time."

Peter smiled. Akela jumped out knee deep

into the water and held the boat. Peter lowered the mainsail and then he and Bill joined Akela in pulling the dinghy ashore.

Peter looked round appreciatively. "Something about an island, isn't there? *Treasure Island, Robinson Crusoe* and all that."

"True enough," said Akela. "All this emptiness only a few miles from the crowds in Bournemouth. It *is* amazing."

Their camping gear was soon ashore and erected. Sausages and beans went down very well for supper. Before long the keen, salt-laden air sent them gratefully to their sleeping bags.

Peter awakened with a start. He blinked and heard Bill's voice. "Going to lie there all day, are you? It's practically mid-day."

"Well, seven-thirty, anyway," came Akela's voice.

The Sixer struggled out of his sleeping bag. He crawled out of the tent and gazed at the early morning sunshine.

"We'll have an early breakfast," said Akela, "and then have a look at another island."

It was not long before they were on the water again. There were very few craft moving at that time of the morning, although there were several scattered about, at anchor, close to the land. This time Akela took the helm, with Peter tending the jib sheets.

"We'll make for that spit of land," said Akela, "by that clump of bushes. There's a path from there leading to a farm. The farmer has let Cub Scouts camp there before, using an old barn, and I would like to take a look."

Soon the boat bumped ashore and Akela jumped ashore. "Look after the dinghy, Peter; Bill and I will walk up to the farm."

"O.K.," said Peter.

The other two started to walk inland and were soon lost to sight. Peter settled himself upon the thwarts. The mainsail had been lowered and the jib flapped gently in the morning breeze. He gazed out across the water at the various craft within sight. There was still little movement but one or two motor craft in the far distance made their ways seawards, and the flash of oars could be seen as a rowing dinghy or two were pulled towards anchored cruisers.

Peter's eye was caught by the motion of one small craft which, moving seaward, would pass fairly closely to him. The Sixer watched idly and then stared intently. The approaching craft had no sails, no plume of water from an outboard engine, and no oars. It contained, however, one figure.

Peter stood up in his dinghy, clutching the mainmast to keep his balance. He could now confirm that, as he had feared, the craft was out of control and drifting down the main channel towards the sea. The figure in the boat waved.

Peter wondered what to do. He looked inland, but there was no sign of Akela and Bill. He glanced at the limp mainsail lying in the boat. He had sailed, he believed, competently in the past, but always under supervision of Akela or another adult. Perhaps it would be wrong to risk a single-handed sail. Also he had to come alongside the drifting rowing boat. He looked at the oars lashed to the bulwarks. This would be more sensible.

Quickly he extracted the rowlocks from the locker and shipped them. He gave a last look ashore and then pushed the dinghy into deeper water. He grasped the oars and pulled steadily on a course which would intercept the drifting craft.

It seemed a long and tedious pull. The dinghy was designed for sailing and was not well designed for rowing.

But he persevered and at last was rewarded by the sight of the craft bobbing along in the grip of the current not far from him. Peter could see the frightened face of a small boy. The Sixer gave a few more strokes and bumped alongside.

"Quickly!" called Peter. "Throw me your painter!"

"What's that?" called the boy.

"That rope; in the bows, the front end," called Peter.

The boy stumbled awkwardly forward and threw Peter the rope. He secured it to the tiller post in the stern of his dinghy.

PUZZLE LETTER

Answer on Page 64

Answer.

Dear Akela,

We are very sorry to hear that you are ill in bed. We do hope you are getting better.

If you like we can come and practice our 1st Aid on you.

Baloo has told us that you have decided on our Summer Camp. We are going to the sea-side.

On Friday we shall be cooking sausages on a camp-fire. We do miss you. Get well soon.

From your Sixers.

"Thanks!" called the boy.

"Where've you come from?" answered the Sixer.

"The motor cruiser *Amanda*."

"The *Amanda*! Were you at Wareham last night?"

"Yes, why?"

"Oh, nothing. Where have you come from now?"

"We came downstream last night and anchored at the mouth of the river. I woke early, left Dad and Mum asleep, and took the boat to go fishing. But I'm not so good at rowing and I lost the oars. Thanks for collecting me."

"It's all right," said Peter. "I'll row back and pick up my friends first."

With that he bent to his rowing and started to pull back to his point of departure.

"You are clever," said the boy. "Where did you learn all this?"

"Oh, in the Cub Scouts."

"Wish I could join them. I'm always asking if I can, but Mum and Dad aren't too keen on the idea."

Peter smiled. "P'raps they can be talked into it somehow."

After a few more strokes the Sixer glanced over his shoulder and realised to his dismay that he was making no progress at all. The combination of two craft made it difficult for him to row against the current. Clearly he could not return immediately to pick up Bill and Akela.

He changed his course slightly and started to pull towards the nearest beach. He pulled steadily but still found himself being carried towards the sea. At last, however, he felt the pull of the current slacken as he left the main stream and began to move through the slack water which bordered the beach.

"Where are we going?" called the young boy staring at the deserted, reedy water's edge.

"No idea," smiled Peter, "but don't worry." With that he bumped lightly aground. "Now," he continued, "*your* boat is better for rowing.

I think I'll beach my dinghy for a spell and I'll try to take you back to your cruiser. But first of all, if you don't mind, I'll take you to Akela and Bill. They are marooned on the beach round the headland."

The boy nodded doubtfully. Peter splashed his way ashore and pulled the sailing dinghy high and dry.

"I think after all," said the boy, "I would rather stop here until Dad comes. I'm afraid I'm a bit scared of that boat."

"O.K., just as you like," said Peter. "I shan't be long. You sure you'll be all right?"

"Oh, yes. I'll stay right here in this boat of yours."

"I'll be off then."

Peter pushed off and recommenced his rowing. He found movement far more easy and, using the slack water, close to the edge, he made rapid progress. He rounded a low-lying headland and could see the figures of Akela and Bill. They were staring out across the water but soon saw Peter and waved.

Peter returned the signal and then turned his back to resume the task of rowing. He had not taken many strokes, however, before he heard the throbbing note of a motor cruiser.

The noise grew louder and he heard the hail: "Hey! You there!"

Peter turned and saw nearby the bulk of an approaching motor cruiser. On the bows was the name *Amanda*. Peter stopped rowing and the craft edged alongside the dinghy. A woman stayed at the wheel while a man leaned over the side and scowled at Peter.

"What are you doing with our tender? We wondered what – what the – you're the young pest who smashed into our cruiser yesterday. I gave you a piece of my mind. Is this what you try to do out of spite?"

"No, it's not that –"

"Don't argue with me. Come aboard!"

A boat hook pulled the dinghy towards the stern of the cruiser and Peter clambered into the well amidships.

The man continued: "Where is my son, Michael? Why are you out here on your own? Where is the man who was with you yesterday?

"I'm trying to explain," said Peter. "Your son's safe. The man, Akela, is over there on the land." The Sixer pointed to the two distant figures. "I'll tell you what happened –"

"You'll tell us what happened when we collect your friends. I want a word with that man of yours. Until then, keep quiet!"

Peter shrugged his shoulders. There was no point in trying to talk to the irate couple. The cruiser soon motored near to the bank and then lay, hove to, with the engine ticking over.

"Hello! You!" called the man. "Come aboard! I've got your lad with me!"

Akela and Bill splashed forwards and waded out to the cruiser. Climbing aboard they were clearly relieved, but puzzled, at the sight of Peter.

Before they could speak the man shouted: "What's going on! We wake up to find my son and the dinghy missing. We're worried stiff and then I find this lad rowing away with our boat. What's your explanation?"

"I don't know," said the mystified Akela. "Why don't you ask Peter?"

"Well, come on then!" said the man. "Out with it!"

"It's like this, you see," said Peter, flustered by the man's manner. "I left your son on the beach when –"

"Oh," said the mother, "you admit you took the boat. D'you hear that! Left poor Michael on a beach! What a wicked boy!"

"I'm sure there's a reasonable explanation," said Akela. "Where did you leave this Michael?"

"Round that headland."

"Right, shall we go and collect him and let him explain," said Akela.

"Good idea!" grunted the father.

Nothing more was said until the *Amanda* rounded the small headland and Michael could be seen waving.

"There he is!" said his mother. "He's all right!"

Soon the boy was aboard and he said. "Sorry I've been so silly, but wasn't it lucky this Cub Scout rescued me."

"He what?" said the father.

Michael explained the episode and then there was a moment's silence.

The father said: "I'm sorry, Peter. I apologise. It sounds as if you have behaved very well indeed." He continued to Akela: "And our apologies to you, too."

"That's all right," said Akela. "I'm sure Peter and I have no hard feelings. You were naturally very worried. I have only one suggestion to make. We can't have Michael in *our* Cub Scouts obviously, but let him join his local Pack if he wants to."

"Oh, yes, please," squealed Michael. "I've been on about that for ages, haven't I?"

"All right," laughed his mother, "we give in."

IN INDIAN COUNTRY

THINGS TO MAKE

To make an Indian teepee (or wigwam) you will need a sheet of cartridge paper 18″ × 10″. If you can't obtain cartridge paper use an old piece of wallpaper which has a plain back.

Mark out shape shown in Fig. 1 with a ruler and a pair of compasses.

Cut out shape.

Roll shape into a cone as shown in Fig. 2.

Glue along overlap, leaving about $1\frac{1}{2}$″ for turning over for door flaps.

Finally, when glue is dry, paint designs on teepee.

For added realism glue a few matchsticks in top opening for the support poles.

TEEPEES

2

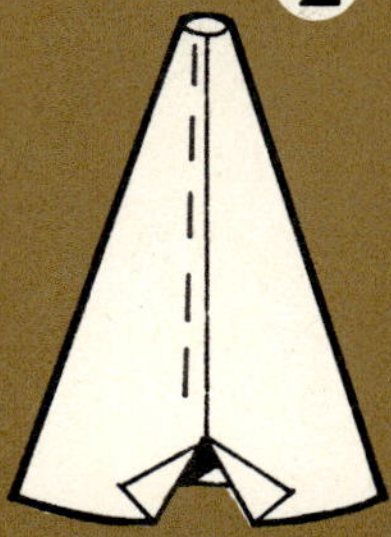

3

1

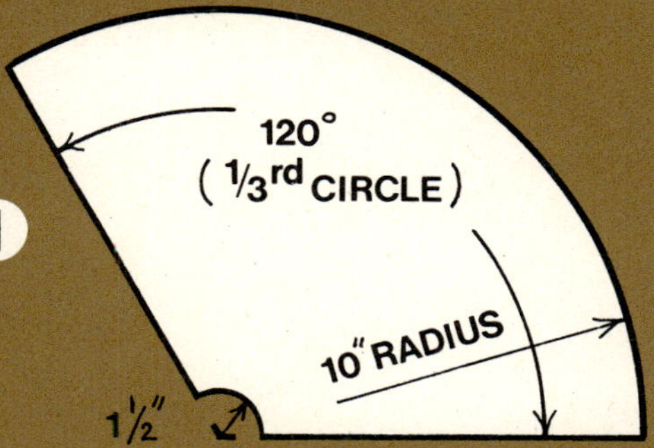

TOTEMS

The totem can be as high as you like. Cut out a number of egg box cones, place these on a piece of card, and cut card to length and width. Glue a triangular support to the back of the card (Fig. 1). Glue on egg box cones (Fig. 2). Add wings from card (Fig. 3). Paint face designs with poster colour paints.

Take a sheet of cartridge paper (or use back of wall-paper), and paint or crayon a background for your Indian Village.

Paint in river, mountains, trees and teepees.

1

2

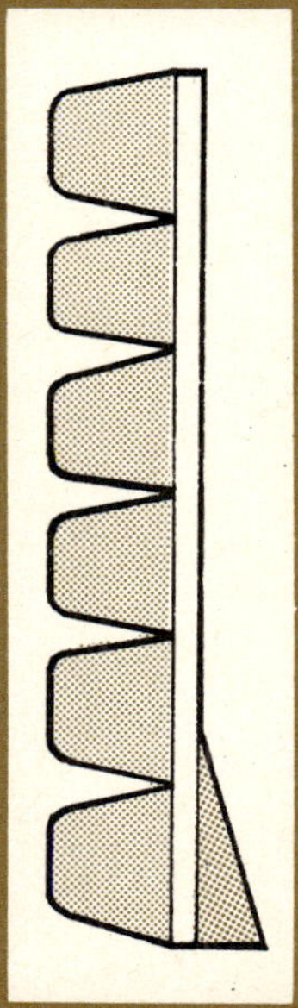

3

PIPE-CLEANER
INDIAN

(a) Cut out an egg box cone, and glue on a piece of card for the face. Trim excess card when glue is dry (Fig. 1).

(b) Paint face. When paint is dry add wool hair, paper headband and paper feather (Fig. 2).

(c) The body is made with pipecleaners. Wind two cleaners to form neck, add a third cleaner for arms, and insert between body members.

Twist arms around body to hold.

Continue to wind body, leaving enough of the body cleaners unwound for legs. (Figs. 3 & 4).

Arrange in required shape, secure to a card base.

Add apron or trousers made from coloured paper (Fig. 5).

1
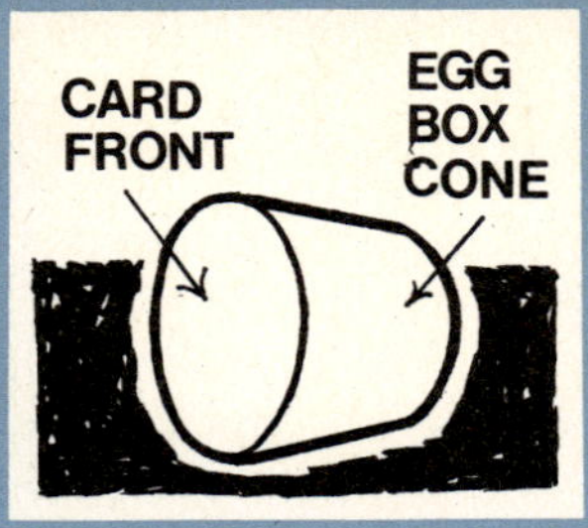

2

3
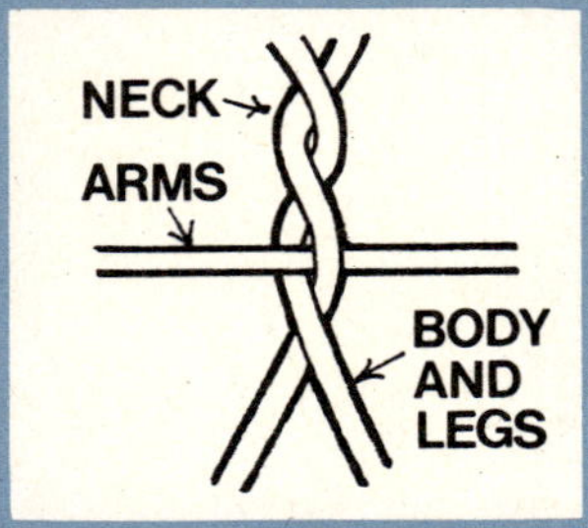

4
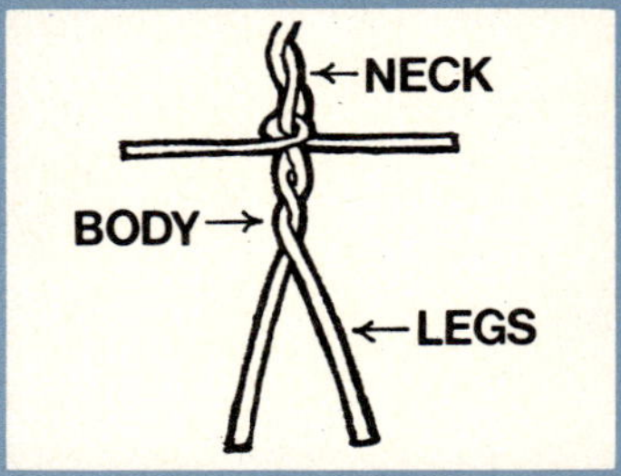

5

NATURE CASTS

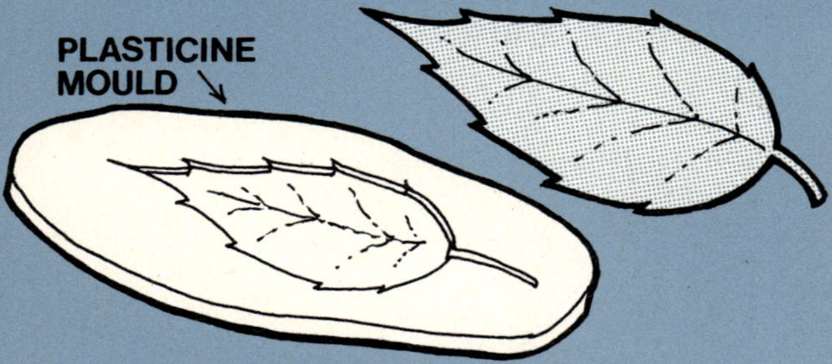

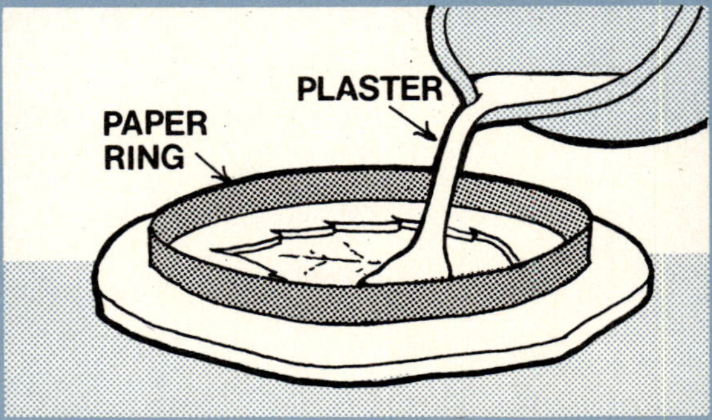

1. Roll out some plasticine.
2. Press a leaf into the plasticine, pressing into the mould with the fingers.
3. Remove the leaf gently.
4. Cut a paper strip about $\frac{1}{2}''$ wide and glue the ends together. The paper ring should be smaller than the plasticine mould.
5. Insert the paper ring into the mould.
6. Mix up some plaster of paris, and pour into the mould.
7. When dry (about 2 hours) remove the plasticine and the paper ring.
8. Paint leaf impression.
9. Clean up mess.

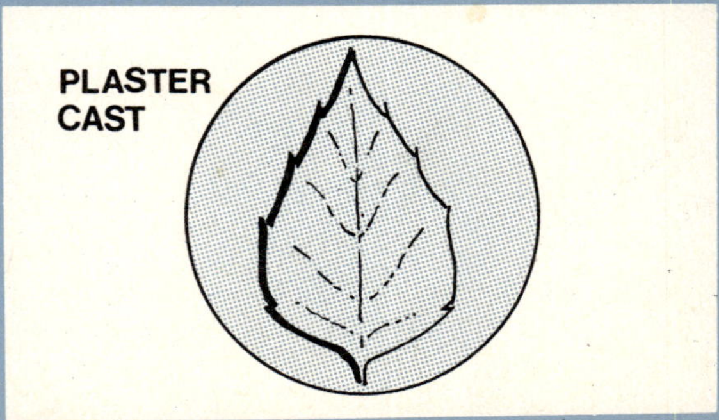

A WALLBOARD TO MAKE

A wallboard is a really useful article: it can be used as a notice-board in the Pack Den, or as a wall panel in your own bedroom for pinning up your pictures and postcards.

To make it all you need is a piece of $\frac{1}{4}$ in. thick pinboard or softboard measuring 3 ft. × 2 ft.; two 5 ft. lengths of $\frac{3}{4}$ in. × $\frac{3}{4}$ in. stripwood; a packet of $\frac{3}{4}$ in. panel pins, and adhesive such as Impact or wood-workers resin adhesive. Here's how to make your panel.

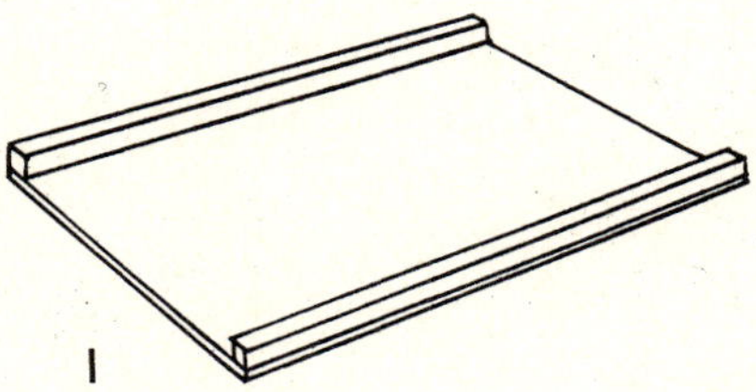

1

Fig. 1. Lay the board down on a level surface, smooth side up, and place one of the lengths of stripwood on top of it, along one of the longer sides. Saw the strip-wood to the exact length of the board, using a junior hacksaw. Cut the second strip in the same way to fit the other long edge of the board. Glue the two strips in place, flush with the edges of the board.

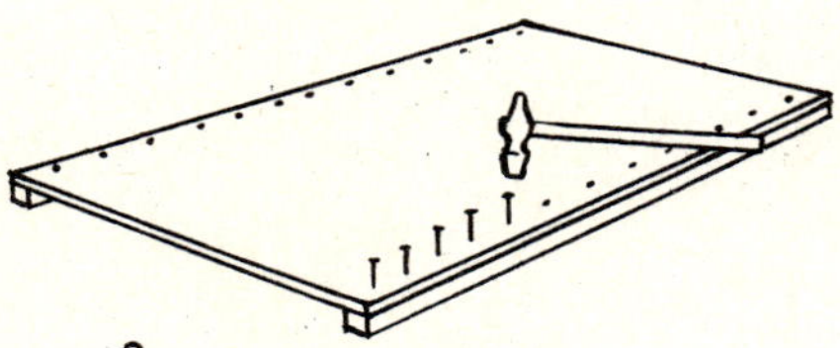

2

Fig. 2. Turn the board over and drive in panel pins at 3 in. intervals to hold the board and strips firmly together.

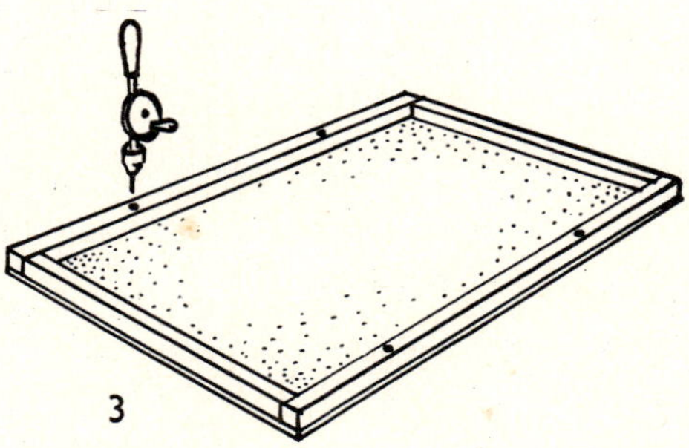

3

Fig. 3. Turn the board face upwards again and use the two remaining pieces of stripwood to line the short edges of the board. Mark the length needed on each piece of stripwood and saw it exactly to size. Glue the two pieces to the board, then turn it over and fix the strips in place with panel pins, as before.

Next, drill four $\frac{1}{4}$ in. diameter holes through the long strips, making each hole 6 in. in from the corner. These holes are for fixing the board to the wall.

Glasspaper the wood smooth, then paint the whole of the board and the wood, using a pale colour of emulsion paint. Two coats will be needed for a good finish.

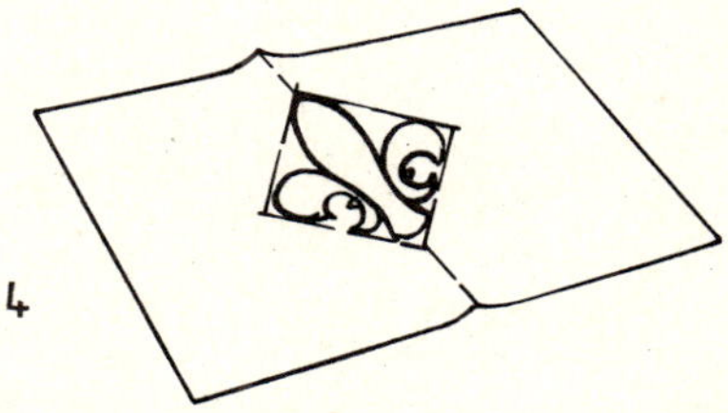

4

Fig. 4. Draw the Scout emblem on a large sheet of thick paper. Make the emblem about 12 in. high and 12 in. wide. The easiest way to do this is to draw a 12 in. square in the centre of the paper as shown, and use this as a guide.

5

Fig. 5. Crease the paper down the centre of the emblem and cut out the half-shape while the paper is held doubled. This will make sure that the final shape is symmetrical.

Lay the cut-out shape in the centre of the board and either draw round it in pencil then paint it in a different colour to that of the board, or stencil the colour on while the paper is in place.

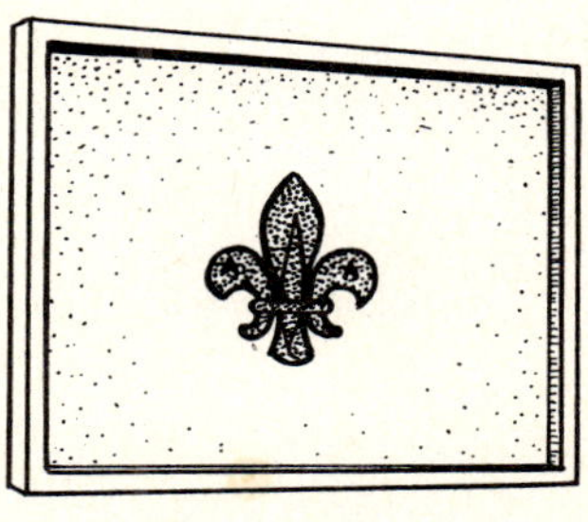

6

Fig. 6. When the paint is dry, draw round the outline of the emblem with a felt-tip pen, or use indian ink and a small brush. This will make it stand out and give your board a very decorative finish.

All that remains now is to fix the board to the wall – masonry pins or screws look neatest, but a loop of nylon cord can also be used. It is best to use map pins to fasten things to your board – they look more decorative than drawing pins, and are easier to pull out again; these can be bought from large stationers.

the arrow trail

You know what an arrow means in tracking? Yes, of course, it means "This is the right way to go. Carry on!"

Perhaps that is why the Cub Scout Tests are called Arrow Tests, because they are pointing the right way to go through Cubbing towards Scouting.

Most of them are fun and everybody enjoys working for them. Because, of course, you must work for them; they wouldn't be worth much if you went through the list saying "Oh, I can do that already", "I know all about that", and "I can tick that off my test card straight away. S'easy".

What about the ones that aren't so easy? That is when everybody asks Akela at once: "Can I do my hank today?"; "What's a forward roll?" and "When can we go exploring?" And Akela tries to plan it all at once so that everybody can have a go at practising what they most want and it's all fun.

But what about the tests that don't seem to be much fun? Some of them tend to be shoved into the background a bit, until somebody says: "What about Health?" and "You don't seem to have done much about Service at Home". Your Test Card looks a bit blank on those lines. Those are the very things which you can tackle on your own, and you'll feel pretty good if you can say to Akela: "I always make my own bed and I can do the corners properly and all"; "Like to see my toe nails? I cut 'em myself and they're super". Or "I telephoned a message for Dad the other day and got it right!"

In the Bronze Arrow tests, 'Germ Warfare' is the one that gets least attention, perhaps because germs are invisible and it's difficult to tackle that sort of enemy. But War is a terrible thing which nobody can ignore. Important? Urgent? It's TOP SECRET PRIORITY!

SECRET AGENTS: FRITZ AND FLITZ

FRITZ was a German who had lived in England for years before the War between England and Germany. Then, of course, he wanted to serve his own country, so he became a spy. He was a waiter in a hotel where all sorts of Servicemen came and went—and *talked,* which is a very dangerous thing to do in wartime, when everybody should keep their mouths buttoned up. Fritz usually managed to be serving them just when they were talking about rather secret things, and they never seemed to notice that the waiter was there, waiting and listening.

"It's the last time I'll be meeting you here," said a sailor to his friend. "We're off tomorrow."

The friend was in R.A.F. uniform, and grumbling:

"You're lucky to get away from this dump. Seems to me we're stuck at Lydd for good."

"But you're Fleet Air Arm, aren't you?"

"Yes, ground crew. But believe me there's plenty of work to keep hundreds of us busy. Servicing all the big kites that are collecting there—you know."

The sailor nodded. "I wish you'd tell your lot to keep a look out for us tomorrow, then. We've got the biggest convoy you ever saw leaving Dover at dawn."

They finished their meal and tipped the waiter, but he had already got the 'tip' he wanted.

Fritz went back to his lodging, got out his secret radio transmitter and set to work with his code book. The British Commander-in-Chief wondered how on earth Hitler knew it would be a good idea to bomb Lydd that night, and to send a lot of U-boat submarines to meet the convoy from Dover in the morning.

All the same we won that war, mostly because we wouldn't give up, and partly because we learnt, after a while, to keep our mouths shut.

FLITZ is another Secret Agent who depends largely on open mouths. He is not a German but a Germ, and he is engaged in endless war against this country. Being invisible is a great help to a spy. His lucky break began when he met Albert, because Albert always breathes through his mouth. Flitz knew that noses were tricky and dangerous, where a spy might get stuck in the anti-germ network of hairs. But Albert was easy, and very soon Albert had a bad cold. He was a Cub and didn't want to miss the Pack Meeting, so he went along, sniffing and coughing.

Right slap in the middle of the Grand Howl he sneezed: "Akela! We'll do our . . . *TISHOO!*"

Most people laughed and so did Flitz. He was shot out into the middle of the circle and had time to choose whom to attack. Of course he went for the most important, and he danced about until Akela opened his mouth to say: "Haven't you got a handkerchief, Albert?"

"It's all right, Akela," said Albert, wiping his nose on his sleeve, in a rather unattractive way he had.

Akela sighed, but it was too late: Flitz had dived headlong into his lungs and was holding on tight.

Three days later Akela was feeling ill. He had to go to the office because he had an important meeting and, as his wife wasn't feeling very well either, he did the shopping for her on the way home. The next day he had to stay in bed with a temperature and three days later dozens of people were ill: all the people Akela had met on the bus, in the office and in the shops.

Flitz had been very busy. His sort of Secret Agent has the wonderful power of being able to multiply as quickly as you can do a sum like $1 \times 4{,}629$. In three days he had produced an army of little Flitzes, all well-trained and sent out to attack the enemy. So many people became ill that shops and businesses were shut, work neglected, money lost; cinemas closed and football matches were cancelled.

It was called a Flu epidemic. Even the schools were closed, which might have been fun if most of the children had not been feeling too ill to enjoy it. Other foreign bodies took the opportunity to attack the weak spots in our defences: some made their headquarters under dirty finger nails, others in teeth that weren't properly cleaned, others infiltrated between dirty socks and dirty feet, and everybody got more and more ill and unable to fight back.

Flitz was triumphant. "The Germans couldn't conquer England," he said, "but we Germs have!"

But England suddenly realised it was in danger of being taken over and, just in time, produced its secret weapons: nail brushes, tooth brushes, scrubbing brushes with lots and lots of ammunition called soap.

Flitz himself, who had become a Field Marshal, got one whiff of antiseptic soap and curled up and died, while all his armies turned tail and fled.

But watch out! There are still lots of Enemy Agents of all sorts hanging about. Englishmen must learn to keep their mouths shut.

interlude for MAGIC

When we think of magic or conjuring tricks, we think mainly of playing cards, or coloured silk handkerchiefs, or perhaps colourful boxes which, after having been shown empty, are suddenly full of sweets or more silk handkerchiefs. But there is another object, not so often seen in this context, which is excellent for magic, and that is – a piece of rope.

Some adults might be suspicious of a Cub Scout who went around with a pack of cards in his pocket, and others might think him a cissy if he had pockets full of silk handkerchiefs, but it is traditional for a boy to have a piece of string in his pocket. This piece of string could well be a bit thicker – a piece of thick cord or thin rope – and, with this simple equipment, he is all set to perform a number of intriguing feats of Magic with Rope.

Now for the best material to use. If you can get a length of soft braid or soft braided nylon cord (or Ulstron cord, which is polypropylene) this is excellent; but it must be soft and flexible. The ends can then be neatly fused in a gas flame. Also excellent is soft cotton rope, the sort that is braided round a straight core: this is what most conjurers use and it can be bought at any magic dealer's shop. The cotton rope should have the ends neatly whipped. The most convenient thickness to look for is rope or cord from about a quarter of an inch in diameter up to three eighths of an inch. For most of the tricks here you will need a piece about thirty inches or so in length. Well, you've got your rope, so now to perform some magic with it.

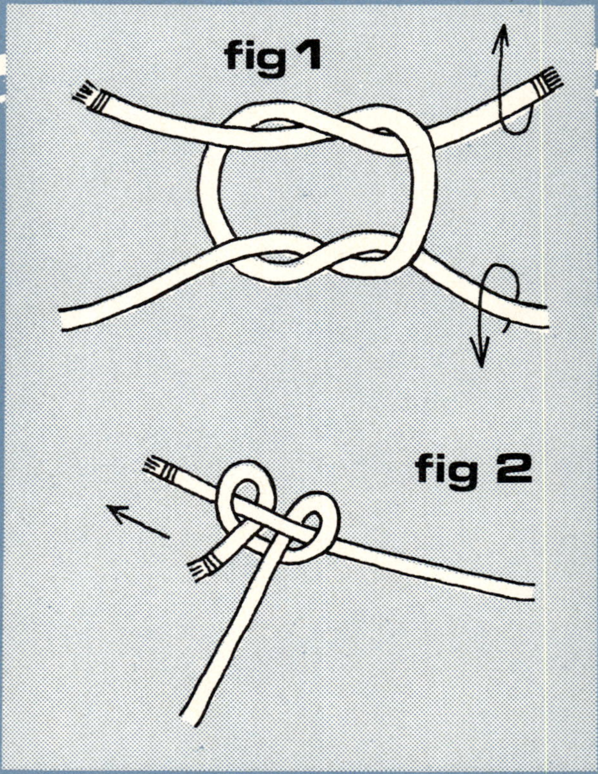

A FIRST TRICK

Most people think that the Reef Knot is one of the firmest and safest of knots, but in actual fact its greatest value is the speed with which it can be untied, and this makes a good trick with which to begin. Tie the two ends of your rope with a reef knot, but don't pull it up too tight (Figure 1). Then, under pretence of pulling it very tight after your audience has seen that it is indeed a Reef Knot, you take hold of one end and the standing part of the same end and pull hard (see the arrows in Figure 1). This has the effect of 'breaking' the knot, which now looks like Figure 2, and one end can be slid off the other.

You must be a bit more mysterious than this, however, so you surreptitiously slide the knot nearer to the end and close one hand over it. With a little practice you will find that you can now push the knot right off the end with the fingers, under cover of the closed fist; it will just look as if you are squeezing away the knot. Then, with a flourish, you say 'Viola!' (or Hey Presto if you haven't started French yet) and toss out the rope – the knot has vanished.

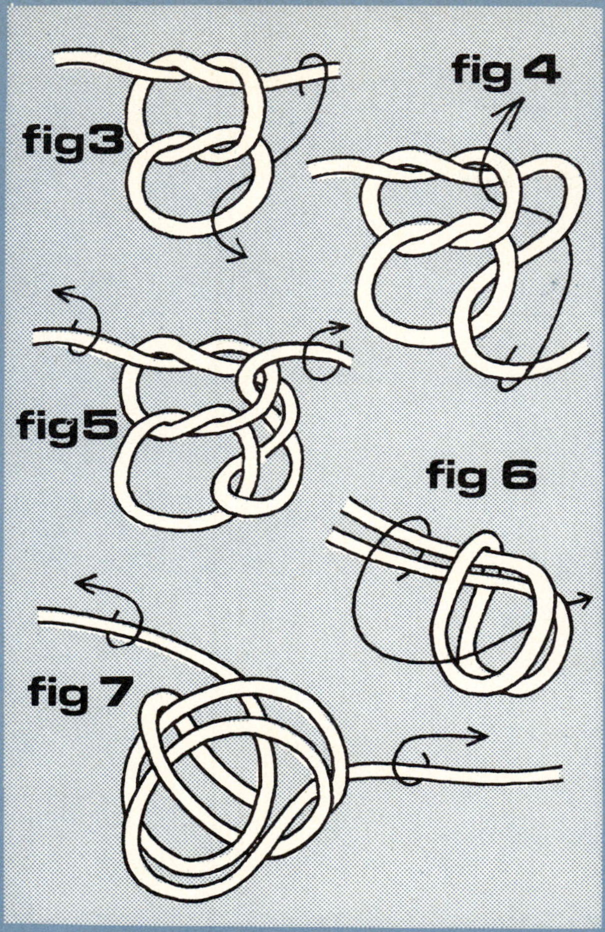

NOW TRY ANOTHER

Some adults, particularly if they are Scouters, or Sailors, may know this trick, of course, but most people in your audience won't. In any case, don't worry, this is only the beginning.

Again tie a Reef Knot but this time leave it well open (Figure 3). Now follow closely Figures 3, 4, and 5. Take the right hand end and put it through the lower bight from the same side: bring it right round to the back and through the centre of the upper bight. Finally, pull gently on the ends until the knot is nearly drawn up in the middle of the rope. Hold this up for a moment or two for everyone to see, and then blow on it, at the same time pulling on the ends. The knot will disappear quite miraculously.

As if that were not enough, you tie another, different knot which also disappears unexpectedly. Fold the rope in two (this is called 'middling the rope'), slip your hand through the bight and take hold of both parts of the rope. Let the bight slip off your hand and you will have the position shown in Figure 6. Pass the two ends through the new bight (see the arrows in Figure 6) and you will have Figure 7. Take hold of the two ends and pull them gently in opposite directions, then you will end up with what appears to be quite a complicated knot: don't pull too hard yet, or you'll bring the trick to a premature end. Hold the rope up for all to see the knot, then blow on it and pull on the ends. Once again the knot will disappear.

THE RE-APPEARING TRICK

So far you have been making knots disappear, but where have they gone? After the last trick, you idly coil up the rope while talking to your audience – I'm afraid it's up to you what you say since I cannot write patter for you.

You are apparently just coiling up the rope as if to put it away, but actually you are coiling it in a very special way. Hold one end of the rope in the left hand, palm upwards. With the right hand, take hold of the rope about six or seven inches from the left hand and put *a reverse loop* over the left hand, as shown in Figures 8 and 9. Repeat this as often as the length of rope will permit, giving you four or five loops (Figure 10). Now put your right hand through all the loops and draw the first end right through. Slowly pull this end up and you will have a series of knots along the length of the rope: you have found the knots which previously vanished – or so your patter can indicate. Figures 11 and 12 show the results.

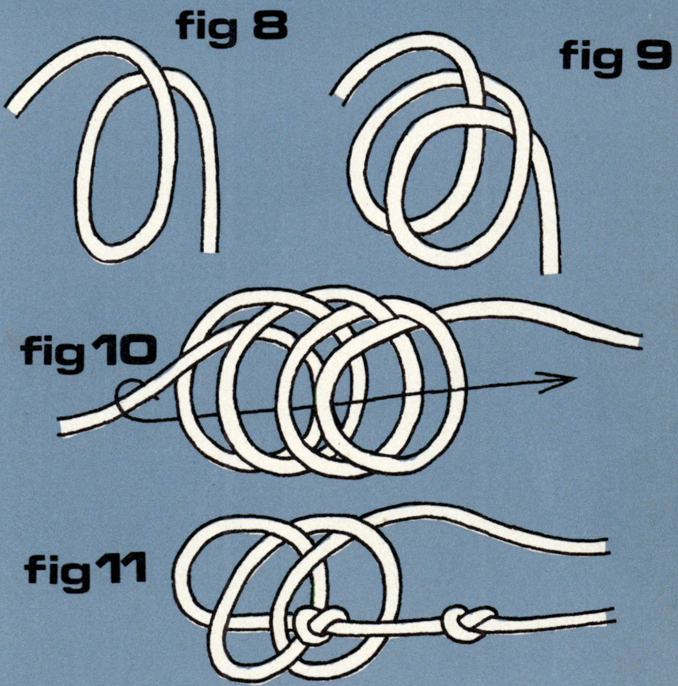

fig 12

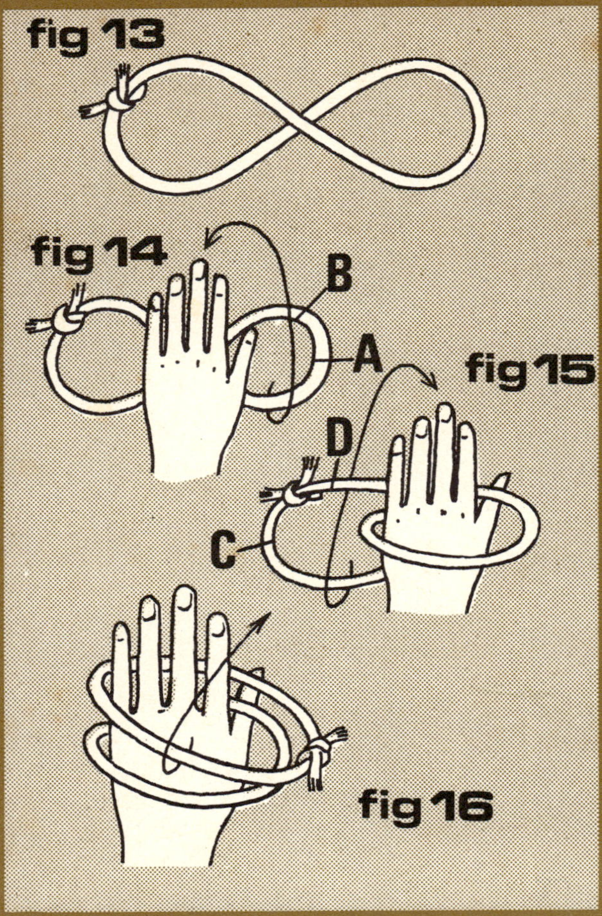

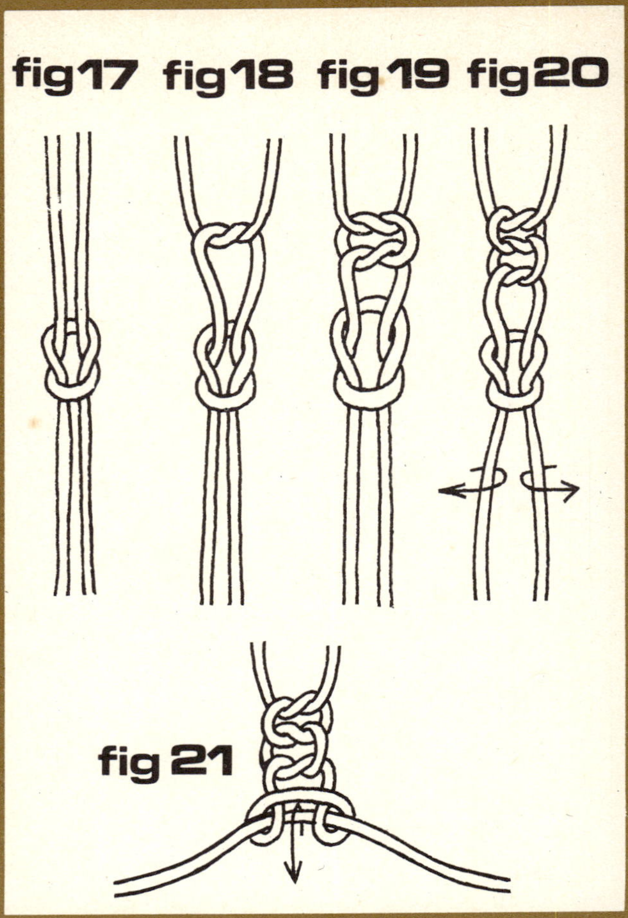

TRY THIS ONE

Now either untie the knots from the last trick or discard that piece of rope and take another, similar piece; tie the two ends together with a Reef Knot. Place the loop you have made on a table in the form of a figure of eight as shown in Figure 13 making sure that the middle members cross exactly as in the drawing and not the reverse way. Place your left hand down over the crossed part (Figure 14). Take hold of the lower right hand loop (A in Figure 14), bring it over the upper part of the loop (B) and under the fingers so that the loop now lies on the back of the hand. Take the lower left hand loop (C) up, under its upper part (D) and under the fingers, leaving another loop on the back of the hand. Keep the left hand pressed down so that no part of the rope will slip out, just lifting the fingers slightly to pass the loops under. Now, pressing down hard with the left hand, take hold of one of the loops on the back of the hand and pull it up, but making it look as if it were hard work. The rope will appear to pass right through your hand, which you leave flat on the table for a moment or two longer. The steps are shown progressively in Figures 13 to 16.

BEFORE YOU TAKE YOUR BOW

For your last trick, take two lengths of rope and tie them together with a Reef Knot *in the middle of the two ropes* (Figure 17) and draw up fairly tight, but not too tight. Let the ropes hang so that everyone can see the knot in the middle. While they are hanging, take the two upper ends and tie a Reef Knot down on to the first knot (Figures 18 and 19).

You can now invite a member of your audience to tie more knots on top of yours. What they will never realise is that the two upper ends with which the knots are tied are the two ends of the same piece of rope. When enough knots have been tied to satisfy everyone, take hold of the two parts of the rope a little below the knots (these are the two parts of the other rope) and pull sideways, (Figure 20); this will break the knot (as you did in the first trick) and you will have the position shown in Figure 21. Holding the assembly in the left hand, take hold of the middle part of the lower rope, which is in the centre of the knot, and pull. The second rope will come away and you have pulled apart the two ropes in spite of all the knots which, apparently, tied them so firmly together.

Who said you had to have cards, silk handkerchiefs or trick boxes to put on a magic show?

Swimming in Safety

"Won't be a minute," shouted Jim as he nipped back to the house. "I just want to get a cutting from tonight's paper."

"What on earth for?" I cried, "if we wait much longer we will miss the bus."

"Never mind, Roy," said Jim. "This is a bit more important than missing the bus."

Even so, it was just the odd minute that made us miss the bus, and as we took the short cut across the park to the Scouts' Meeting he was full of apology.

"Don't worry," I said, "the walk will do us good, but I wanted to be early tonight to hear that talk on swimming by the Badge Examiner, and to ask him what he thinks of my little scheme for next week's camp at Northsea."

"I know," said Jim. "that's what the cutting's about. Fancy 1000 deaths a year from drowning in Britain alone."

Poor Jim needed no reminding of this tragedy of bathing accidents since his own father had been drowned in a gallant but unsuccessful attempt to rescue a foolhardy youth who had persisted in swimming alone from a dangerous part of a beach in spite of clear warning notices of dangerous tides.

I was suddenly awakened from my thoughts by an agonising cry of 'HELP' from the direction of the park pond.

As Jim and I sprinted across the grass our eyes soon became riveted on a petrified youth, clinging to the side of a half submerged raft and shouting "HELP! HELP!"

"What's the matter?" Jim and I cried in unison.

"It's my kid brother," answered the youth. "He's slipped off the raft and I can't swim."

"Where is he?" I asked, as I kicked off my shoes and quickly shed my Scout's uniform.

"In that clear patch beyond the water lilies," he whimpered.

Without more ado I told Jim to call help, while I plunged into the water, struggling to clear the old bedraggled water lilies that clung to my arms and legs.

Once clear of the obstruction, I soon righted the raft, and taking a deep breath I dived downwards into the murky waters. Fortunately, it was not very deep, otherwise I'm sure I would never have seen the body which I found by touch in the dark waters of the pool.

As I made the surface with the limp body, the youth on the home-made raft had gathered some of his composure, but could only ask: "Is he dead?"

"I don't know," I answered, "but pull him on the raft."

And as I turned to push the raft through the water lilies towards the bank I saw the welcome sight of Jim with the Park Keeper.

"How is he?" asked Jim, as he threw out a stout rope which I tied to a broken plank in the raft.

"Can't tell," I replied as Jim pulled in the raft, "but we need to get him to the bank and try artificial respiration."

Thanks to his Scouting first aid knowledge, Jim soon brought back the first flickering signs of life to the limp body, and as the ambulancemen who had been hastily summoned by the Park Keeper's wife took over, they told us he was probably out of immediate danger.

"Come on," shouted the ambulancemen as they made the casualty warm and snug in the ambulance, "get these blankets wrapped round you, and let's see what the Doctor has to say."

And as I and the youth wrapped ourselves in the warm blankets, Jim picked up my togs and we all drove straight to the local hospital.

The Casualty Doctor wasted no time in learning the full details from the victim's brother, and after checking that the youngster was the only one in need of treatment Jim and I were thanked for our prompt actions and sent to my home by ambulance.

The police, who had been given full details of the happening, immediately notified our parents and the Scout Leader, Mr. Jenkins, and almost before I had time to finish my hot bath and join Jim, who had been giving my parents details of what happened, Mr. Jenkins and the Badge Examiner were ringing the door bell.

"Come in," said my Dad as he opened the door, "it's been quite an evening. We're just having a cup of tea; care to join us?"

It was indeed a pleasant little gathering, and

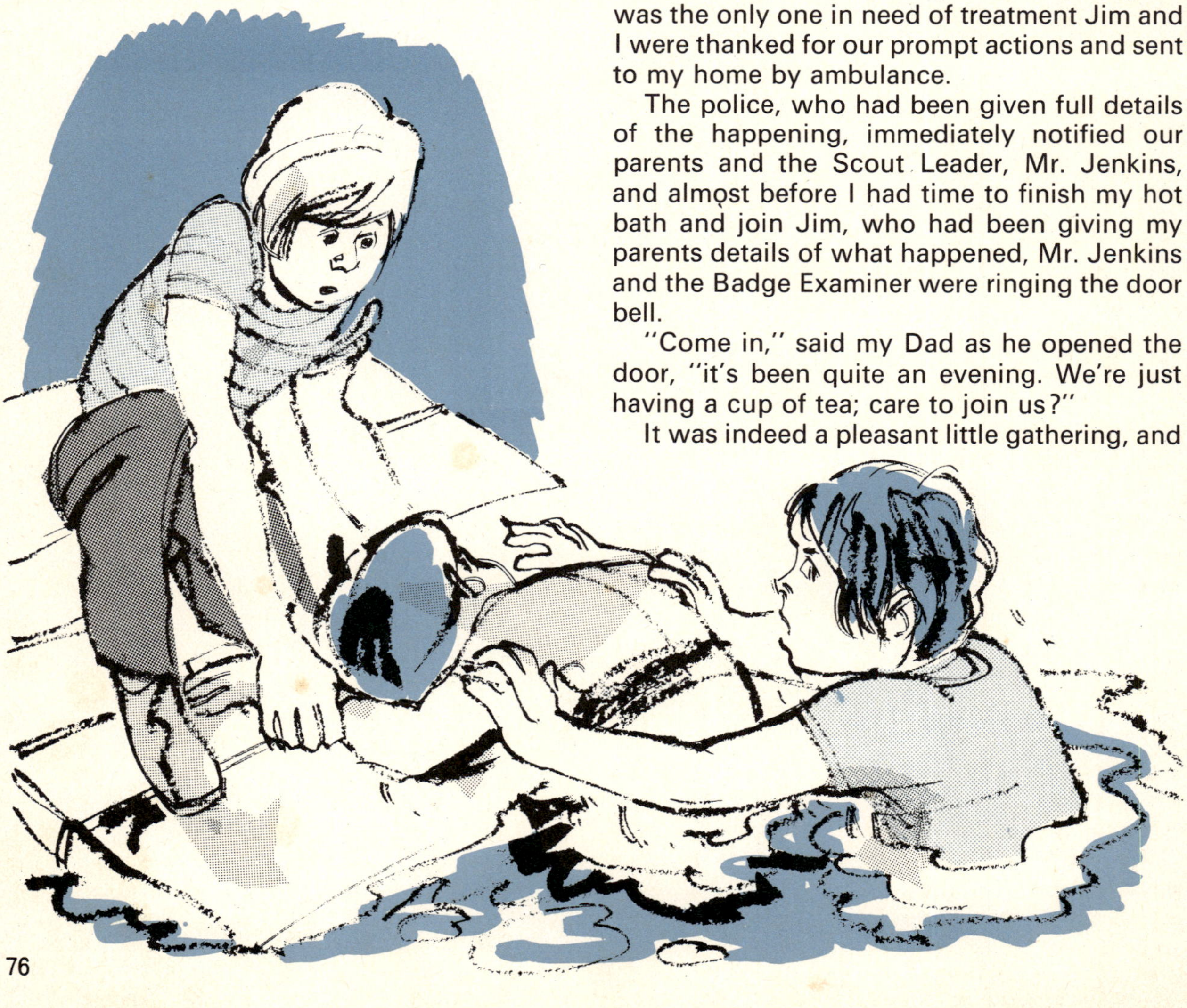

Make a magic wallet.

Materials

4 pieces of cardboard covered with patterned paper on one side.

Size about 4½ in. × 3 in.

4 pieces of white tape about 6 in. long each.

Paste.

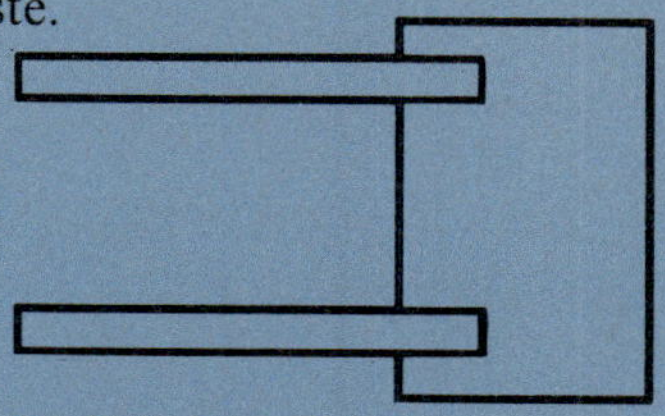

Method of Assembly

1. Place cardboard on table with patterned side downward. Paste the end inch of two pieces of tape and stick them as shown in Fig. 1.

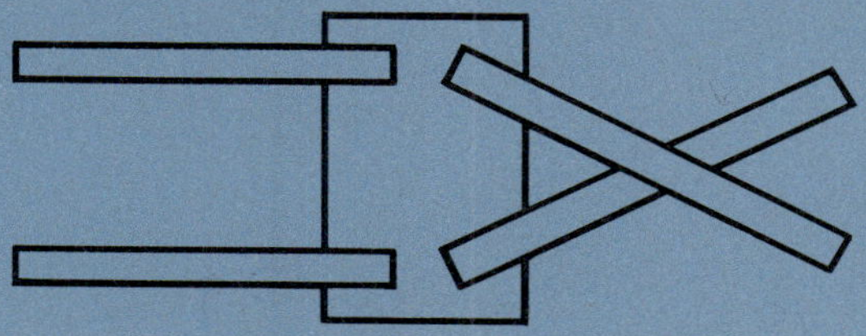

2. Paste the end inch of the other two pieces of tape, and stick as in Fig. 2.

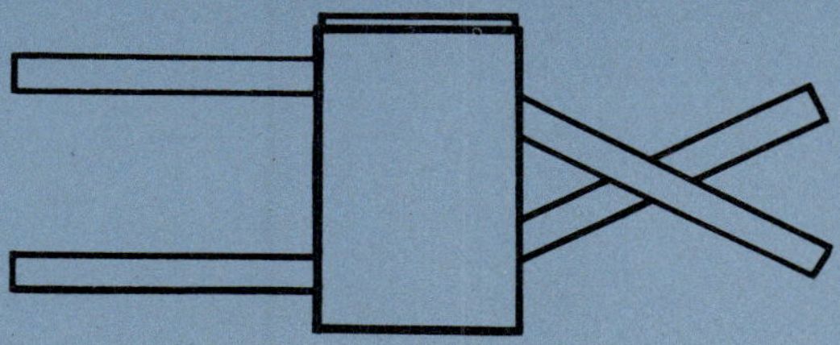

3. Paste another piece of card above card 1, pattern side upwards. (Fig. 3.)

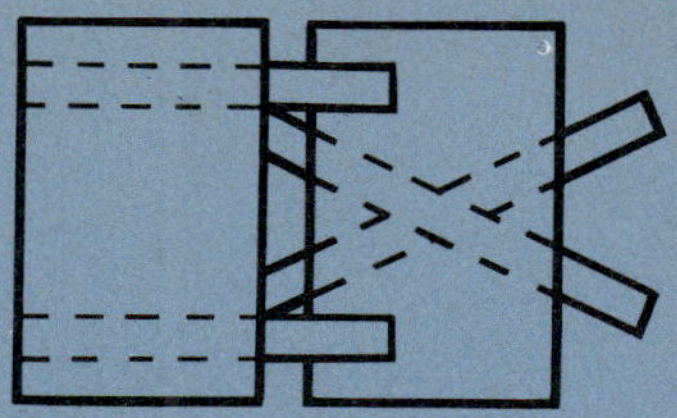

4. Place a third piece of cardboard pattern side downwards, close to the first two – having folded tapes as shown – but not pasted. (Fig. 4.)

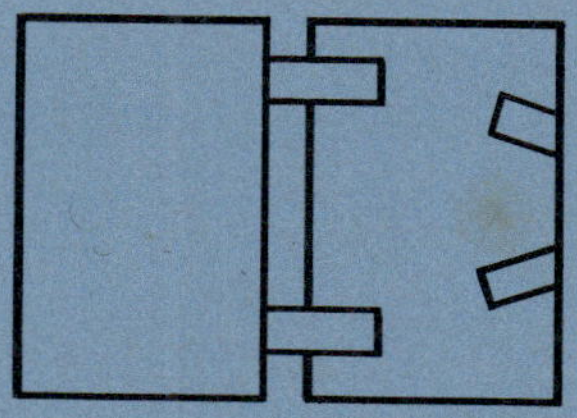

5. Paste end of tapes onto third board. (Fig. 5.)

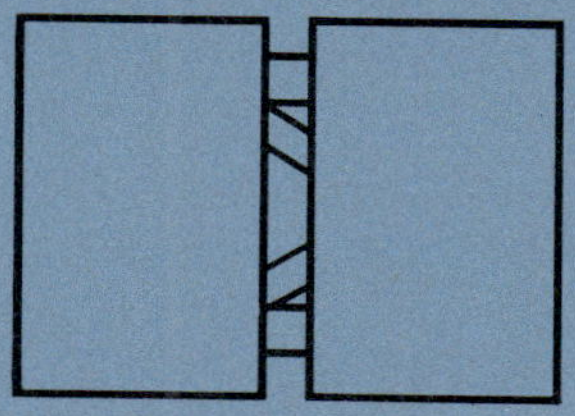

6. Cover tapes with fourth board. (Fig. 6.)

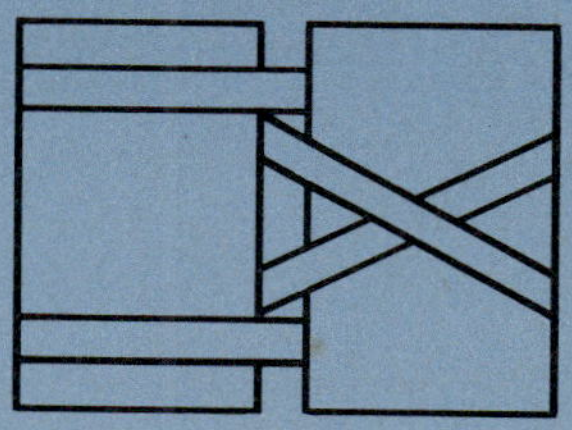

7. Turn wallet over. (Fig. 7.)

Place a photograph under the tapes on one side of the wallet, close and open from the other side. Watch the photo and the tapes. Magic!!

the Badge Examiner, who was an ex-Navy man, was quite a story-teller.

He had been in the Navy during the war and told us of a rather drastic teaching method practised by one of the 'Old Sea Dogs' with Navy Volunteers – although I understand the method was soon banned.

"Now, my lads," the Old Sea Dog would say as he had the Volunteers lined up along the edge of the baths in underpants and vests. "Who can't swim?"

If anyone was bold enough to admit it, he would bellow back: "And how do you know, lad, have you ever tried?"

The replies varied, but the treatment was the same. If the Volunteer said "Yes" he was pushed into the water with the loud cry of "Well, have another try."

If he said "No" he was pushed in to the cry of: "Well, have a try now."

It is only fair to relate that there was never a fatal accident. There were always enough trained men on hand to ensure that everyone was hauled out safely. In fact, the system had a high rate of success, but it was the failures that provided a serious problem.

Some of the young men would possibly be afraid of water for the rest of their lives, and many were obliged to transfer to another branch of the Armed Services, but he said it taught him his most important lesson – NEVER PANIC.

"You see," he said, "swimming is easy. If people would just keep calm, and move their

Stand clear if you meet Bracknell Cub Scout David Barnes; he is the junior champion pea shooter, having successfully shot a pea 43 feet 8 inches!

arms and legs they would stay afloat. In fact it's almost as easy as walking."

Not all dogs like water, but most of them do, and they just go straight off the sands into the sea, moving their paws in exactly the same way, and you seldom hear of a dog drowning, except in very rough waters.

"Anyway," said the Badge Examiner, "it's getting late now, so we will say cheerio. But don't worry, that was a grand idea you had for next week's camp, and Mr. Jenkins has fixed it all up with Northsea's Publicity Manager."

As Jim and I led the Troop from Northsea station the following week, we were greeted by a large Notice Board over the EXIT, which read:

NORTHSEA OFFERS SAFE BATHING, BUT DON'T TAKE OUR WORD FOR IT. JOIN THE 99th BATTALION SAFE SEA BATHERS, AND PROVE IT FOR YOURSELF.

The wording caught the rest of the Troop so much by surprise that they were almost lost for words.

"Say, who's idea was this – we are the 99th, aren't we?" they asked amongst themselves.

The words were no sooner out of their mouths when their eyes caught another notice less than fifty yards ahead.

WHEN THE FLAGS ARE
FLYING RED
DAVY JONES PREPARES
YOUR BED,
WHEN THE FLAGS ARE
FLYING GREEN
FATHER NEPTUNE SMILES
SERENE.

Very good, I thought, Mr. Jenkins had certainly been quick on the ball, and arranged everything perfectly, and the final notice clinched it.

JOIN THE SCOUTS AND LEARN TO SWIM. PLEASE WATCH THE PIER HEAD NOTICE BOARD FOR PLACES AND TIMES.

"Well," said Mr. Jenkins, breaking into my thoughts, "welcome to Northsea. I'm sure you will all be pleased to know that it was Roy's idea to promote 'Safety First in Swimming', and the Publicity Manager and all Northsea Council will co-operate one hundred per cent. The Town Council will advertise the Bathing Parties at a time and place when the beach is safe."

I'm sure that most parents will be delighted to know that they can relax in the knowledge that there will always be help on hand from the Sporting 99th.

The Compass can be Fun

A compass game based on an exciting adventure story can be fun as well as instructive for Cubs who are just learning the art of orienteering.

First draw a plan, either of your own area or of a fictitious town or island. Mark on this plan landmarks and places of interest.

If you wish to make this into a competitive team game draw several identical plans with a different indication for North on each, giving each plan an identifying code letter to make answer-checking easy.

On a separate sheet set out a list of movements. The Cubs work out from their plans the direction of each movement. The team with the most correct answers wins.

List the correct answers to the questions for each movement and each plan. Answers may be given between each question so that the Cubs may have a second chance if they make a mistake.

Make the story as exciting as possible. The following example will show how simply and briefly this may be achieved.

1. Bert moored his boat at Shark Quay and walked to the Jolly Roger Inn.
2. He then went to Harry's House.
3. They both went to Fred's Fried Fish Shop.
4. There they met Sam who had moored his boat in Tiger Bay. They all went down to the Wishing Well.
5. Sam made a wish and he heard a voice from the bottom of the well say, "Go to Pete's Point". So they all went.
6. There they met One Legged Will, who took them to Pirate's Peak.
7. They went to the side of the hillside nearest to Walrus Island. They saw an arrow marked out in stones pointing towards Parrot's Palm. They followed the arrow.
8. A green, talking parrot told them to walk twelve paces towards the lighthouse and start to dig. They find a large treasure chest full of diamonds, rubies and gold.

TREASURE ISLAND

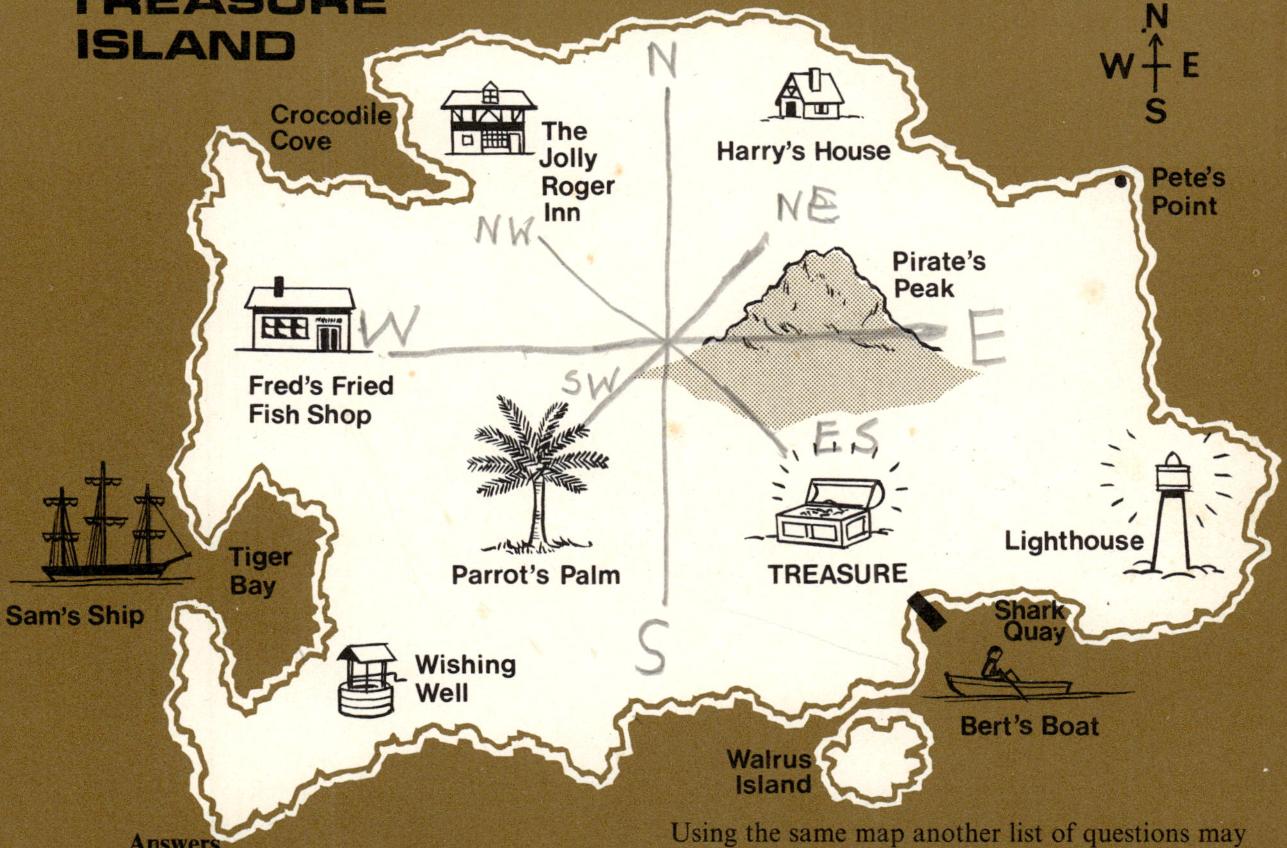

Answers

1. N.W. 2. E. 3. S.W. 4. S.
5. N.E. 6. S.W. 7. S.W. 8. E.

Using the same map another list of questions may be compiled substituting compass directions for movements. The Cubs identify the places arrived at by following these directions.

ADVENTURE IN THE ATTIC

Alan looked at his Job Card. Cutting the grass, sweeping paths, weeding, fetching coal and running errands were some of the jobs he had down so far.

This Scout Job Week was very hot work. He wished someone would find him a nice sitting-down job for a change!

Wonder what I'll get next, he thought, knocking on yet another door.

An elderly man carrying an armful of old newspapers opened the door.

"Scout Job Week!" he said, looking at Alan's Job Card. "Nay, lad, I'm sorry – but I can't afford it. Try next door. Mrs. Turner might find you something."

Alan looked at the newspapers.

"Are those for throwing away? I'll put them by the dustbin for you, if you like."

"That's very good of you, lad. My legs aren't what they used to be. Trying to clear out the attic I am. Be blowed if I couldn't do with one of them lifts to get me up the stairs."

Alan put the newspapers in a cardboard box he found beside the dustbin, and went back to the old man.

"Would you like me to help you clear out the attic?" he asked. "Not for my job," he added quickly. "It can be my good turn for today."

The man's face brightened.

"I'd be pleased of a bit of help, that I would," he said. "Come in, lad, come in."

Alan followed him into a tiny kitchen.

"Sit yourself down," said the old man, pointing to a small stool in the corner. "You look fair hot and bothered."

He poured something into a glass and handed it to Alan.

"There, drink that. There's nothing like a glass of cold ginger beer on a hot day."

Alan sipped at it gratefully.

"Wouldn't be without my ginger beer, I wouldn't. My daughter brings me some each week."

The old man settled himself slowly into a chair.

"Wish she lived nearer. She's over at Churleigh. It's as much as she can manage on a Sunday, what with her family and all."

He looked across at Alan.

"So you're a Wolf Cub, are you?" he asked.

"Well – we used to be Wolf Cubs," replied Alan, "but now we are known as Cub Scouts."

"Are you now? I had a younger sister who used to be in the Rosebuds. Always remember that name because my father used to grow roses at the time," chuckled the old man. "They changed their name to Fairies or Brownies or some suchlike, didn't they?"

"Brownies, Mr. ——er?"

"Aye, I'm sorry, lad. Powell's my name. What's yours?"

"Alan Dale."

"Well, Alan, if you've finished your ginger beer, we'll be off upstairs."

In the attic Alan stared in amazement at the huge collection of things.

There must have been hundreds of newspapers, together with dusty pictures, old trunks, suitcases, a broken umbrella stand, piles of old records, and goodness knows what else.

Mr. Powell laughed when he saw Alan's face.

"It's a right jumble, isn't it? Just goes to show what you collect over the years."

Alan nodded.

"It was all right when the missis was here, God rest her," went on Mr. Powell. "Used to keep everything in order, she did. But now . . ." he smiled ruefully.

"Shall I start by taking some more newspapers down?" asked Alan.

"Aye, lad, if you will. I'll put 'em in piles for you."

STOP PRESS

We have heard of Cub Scouts of all nations and creeds but never 'Donkey Cubs'! But they have them in Devon! The 6th Exeter John Stocker Scout Group enlisted a herd of donkeys to help them raise money for their new Headquarters. They were soon taken over by the Cubs at the afternoon's 'Donkey Dilemma' held in the grounds of the Royal School for the Deaf.

It wasn't long before Alan had his Cub jersey off. Trailing up and down the stairs so many times was far harder work than he had thought.

At last, however, the newspapers were all stacked neatly by the dustbin. The umbrella stand and a pile of broken records soon joined them.

"Dunno what to do about the pictures, though," said Mr. Powell, scratching his head. "I shan't be wanting 'em again, but it seems a waste to throw 'em away."

"I'll take them to the Church Hall if you like," offered Alan. "The Scouts are having a Jumble Sale soon and they could put them in that."

"That's settled, then," said the old man. "We'd better dust 'em though. There's a duster downstairs in the kitchen cupboard."

Alan went to open the door. He must have pulled too hard, for the knob came off in his hand.

"Don't mind that, lad," said Mr. Powell, seeing Alan's worried look. "Been meaning to fix that for ages. I just don't seem to get around to it, with it being for a junk room like. Push it back on the bar sticking through the door, and it will open."

Soon Alan was back with the duster and a brush and shovel he had found in the cupboard.

They dusted the pictures and swept the floor, and then all that remained to do was pull out an old trunk from a narrow alcove. The trunk was covered by a dust sheet and, as they moved it, something slid from under the sheet and dropped with a slight plop on the floor.

"Now, what can that be, I wonder?" said Mr. Powell.

Alan picked up a stiff envelope.

"Have a look inside, will you, lad?" said Mr. Powell. "I haven't got my glasses."

Alan opened the envelope and took out a small thin book. He shook the envelope, but there was nothing more inside.

"What is it, lad?" asked the old man, peering over his shoulder.

"It looks like a bank book of some kind," replied Alan, opening the book.

"Nay, can't be one of them. I don't hold with banks."

"It is, Mr. Powell." Alan's voice rose in excitement. "It is, and . . ." he stopped, his eyes widening.

"And what, lad?" Mr. Powell was screwing up his eyes trying to read the book.

"There's . . . there's three hundred pounds in it," gasped Alan.

"Three hundred pounds," echoed the old man. "You must have made a mistake, lad. I've never had three hundred pounds in my life."

"Well, you have now, Mr. Powell. Look!" The boy thrust the book under Mr. Powell's nose. He peered at it closely.

"Eh, you're right, you know," said the old man at last. "I can just make out the 3, and are them the two 0s?" Mr. Powell's finger pointed to the figures shakily.

"Yes, they are," cried Alan, hopping about in excitement. "Oh, Mr. Powell, you're rich."

Mr. Powell sank down on to a suitcase.

"Well, you've right bowled me over, you have," he said weakly. "Three hundred pounds. It's a fair bit of money, is that."

He looked up as a thought struck him.

"Alan, there'll be a name on it somewhere. Just have a look, will you?"

"Yes, there is," said Alan. "It's Sarah Powell."

"Sarah," repeated the old man softly. "Yes, it would be. Just like my Sarah, that is. Kept saying she'd start putting something by for a rainy day, as she called it, but I never knew she'd done it."

He sighed and stood up unsteadily.

"I'd better put this somewhere safe."

He went to the door and something dropped to the floor.

"Deng it. I've done it myself now," he cried, picking up the door knob.

With shaking hands he attempted to put it on the bar, but in doing so pushed the bar out of the door. There was a muffled clatter as the bar attached to the other knob fell outside the door.

"Ee, that's done it, lad."

"Why, what's wrong, Mr. Powell?" asked Alan.

Mr. Powell held up the loose door knob.

"We're locked in, that's what," he said.

"What are we going to do?" Alan asked him.

"Dunno, lad, unless we can fish the knob in from the other side. That one is still fastened to the bar, and we could use it from this side."

After many attempts they managed to get the bar under the door, but there wasn't enough space for the knob to come through.

"Well, that way's no good," said Mr. Powell at last.

"I know," cried Alan. "We'll try the window."

"We can't get out of that," Mr. Powell said in alarm, looking at the small window set in the sloping roof.

"No, but I can shout and attract someone's attention," said Alan.

He pushed some suitcases beneath the window and climbed on top of them.

"Bother! The window's stuck," he cried, after several attempts to open it.

"Here, let me have a go," said the old man, and he began to shove hard at the window.

But the window remained fast.

"Perhaps if we both push together it will unstick itself," suggested Alan.

They tried this and suddenly the window opened, showering them with dust and bits of flaking paint.

When Alan looked out he could see the opposite side of the street. There was a butcher's shop on the corner, with an awning shading its window. As he watched, two cars went by, and then a lady stopped by the shop. He shouted as loudly as he could.

"Help! Help!"

The lady turned and stared about her.

"Help!" shouted Alan again.

But the lady didn't see him high up in the roof, and she went on down the street.

A boy on a bicycle was the next to come by.

"Hi! You down there!"

The boy looked behind him and wobbled. He couldn't see anyone either and pedalled off round the corner.

Mr. Powell had a try at shouting, but his voice wasn't as strong as Alan's, and no one heard him at all.

Then Alan remembered his Job-Done stickers in his pocket. He had given a number out to people to stick on their windows and doors, but he still had quite a lot left.

"Have we any paper I could write on?" he asked Mr. Powell.

"There's only this 'ere envelope," said Mr. Powell, passing him the envelope which had contained the bank book.

"Thank you. Now, what's the number of your house, Mr. Powell?"

"It's forty-six, lad. What are you trying to do?"

"I'll show you in a minute," replied Alan.

He then tore the envelope in half and on one half he wrote:

HELP. ATTIC. No. 46

He stuck two of his yellow labels end to end to form a tail, and fastened this to his note.

"Now, I'll wait until someone comes along the street and throw the note out of the window," he told Mr. Powell.

Eventually another lady turned into the butcher's shop. Alan waited until he saw her in the doorway again and threw out his note.

It slid down the roof and lodged in the gutter. The boy and the old man watched it

a crossword puzzle

CLUES ACROSS.

1. Device for leading wild birds into a snare.
3. These are scored in Rugby.
6. These occur in Tennis.
8. The score of nothing.
9. Mark aimed at in games like Quoits or Bowls.
10. A 'Weight' in Boxing.
11. There is a World one awarded in Football.
12. Useful hint about betting odds.
16. Cricketer at the wicket.
17. Contest of wrestling by Cowboys and Steers.
18. Tennis score of forty all.

CLUES DOWN.

1. Games not won or lost.
2. A famous cricket ground in London.
4. Piece of Angling equipment.
5. Kind of Sword used in Fencing, of Hungarian origin.
7. Football clubs are divided up into these.
11. The famous Braemar one weighs 230 lbs.
13. Name given to money earned by a Boxer.
14. An athlete tries to reach this first.
15. A kind of Fish.

ANSWERS

ACROSS

1. DECOY. 3. TRIES. 6. RALLIES. 8. NIL. 9. TEE. 10. LIGHT. 11. CUP. 12. TIP. 16. BATSMAN. 17. RODEO. 18. DEUCE.

DOWN

1. DRAWN. 2. OVAL. 4. REEL. 5. SABRE. 7. LEAGUES. 11. CABER. 13. PURSE. 14. TAPE. 15. DACE.

anxiously. Fortunately a light breeze lifted it and it disappeared over the edge.

The lady emerged from the shop followed by the butcher. The man remained standing at his door after his customer had turned the corner of the street.

Alan began to shout loudly. The butcher looked up and down the street.

"Here! I'm up here!" bellowed Alan, and began to wave his white scarf frantically.

The butcher looked up and saw the scarf waving. He smiled and waved back, then turned as if to enter his shop again.

"Help! Help! Don't go in!" shouted the boy.

The butcher hesitated and looked up again. As he did so, Alan's note fluttered down to the road.

The man saw it and picked it up. He turned it over in his hands and read the message.

A few minutes later and the butcher was letting them out of the attic.

"Gosh, I thought we were never going to get out," gasped Alan, as he and Mr. Powell thanked the man.

"Aye. I was beginning to think that myself," said Mr. Powell. "My first job when we've had some tea is to fix that handle!"

The following week Alan handed in his Job Card, together with the money he had earned.

Akela booked it down, and then took a letter from her pocket and read it to the Pack:

Dear Cub Leader,

I'd like to tell you that Alan Dale did a job for me for nothing when he knew I couldn't afford to pay him. Next he found me a bank book I didn't know existed. To cap the lot, when we got locked in he had us rescued.

He's a grand lad and if all your lads are like him, you've a fine bunch.

Now I've got some money will you give the enclosed to Alan for his Job Card.

Joseph Powell.

Alan went red in the face and shuffled his feet uncomfortably, as Akela handed him the money.

"Five pounds," he gasped. "Gosh, that's a lot of money."

Akela smiled as she added it to his total.

"Mr. Powell thinks you earned it," she told him.

From the cheering going on in the Den, everyone else must have thought so too!

LANARKSHIRE LARKS

Lanarkshire Cub Scouts' Open Day

From a contribution by Rob Steele

10th June was 'D Day' for hundreds of Lanarkshire Cub Scouts when they attended the finals of the Annual County Competition held at Crossbasket near East Kilbride. This year the competition took the form of a Pack exhibit showing nature through the seasons. District heats were held and the winners went forward to the finals – which in fact became a day of fun, adventure and competitions.

Fifty pence a Pack and 10p a Cub was all that was needed for an Open Day badge; an open sesame ticket for pony rides, archery, hoop-la, golf, bowls, plate smashing, water pistol competitions, fishing for mousetraps and an aerial runway. By one o'clock the Crossbasket Site was echoing with the shouts and laughter of the excited Cubs. The stalls were in full swing and many had found the Aunt Sally, where the queue of boys waiting to poke their faces through the hole to become the target for the large soggy sponges was longer than the queue of waiting throwers!

Five-a-side football on three pitches and a mini Olympics Stadium with fourteen events were alive with Cubs throughout the afternoon. The boys worked off their energy in pillow fights, water shooting with filled polythene spray bottles as 'guns', equestrian events, running, jumping and generally rushing around.

At 5 p.m. Akelas and Leaders were rounding up their charges, who departed unwillingly with their 'gold' and 'silver' medals around their necks and their pockets stuffed with sweets which they had won at the side-shows. Some tired, some cheeky and some chirpy, but all happy and smiling, especially 1st Baillieston Pack who had won the County Competition with their well prepared exhibit.

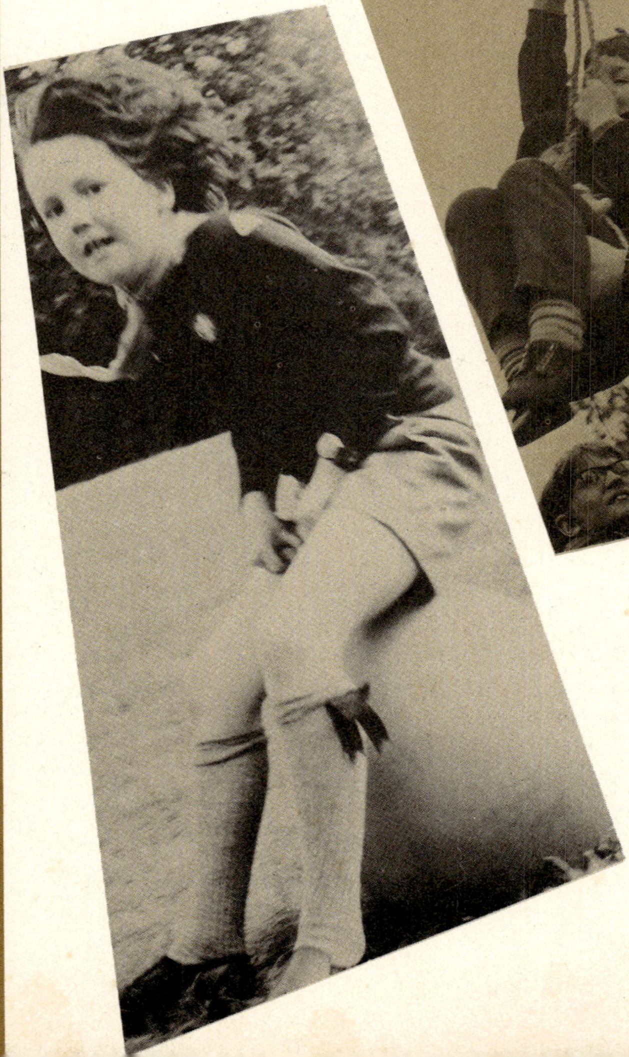